A HISTORY OF SCARS

— A Memoir —

LAURA LEE

ATRIA PAPERBACK

New York London Toronto Sydney New Delhi

An Imprint of Simon & Schuster, Inc.
1230 Avenue of the Americas
New York, NY 10020

First Atria Paperback edition March 2021

ATRIA PAPERBACK and colophon are trademarks of Simon & Schuster, Inc.

For information about special discounts for bulk purchases, please
contact Simon & Schuster Special Sales at 1-866-506-1949 or
business@simonandschuster.com.

The Simon & Schuster Speakers Bureau can bring authors to your live
event. For more information or to book an event, contact the Simon &
Schuster Speakers Bureau at 1-866-248-3049 or visit our website at
www.simonspeakers.com.

Interior design by Jill Putorti

Manufactured in the United States of America

1 3 5 7 9 10 8 6 4 2

Library of Congress Cataloging-in-Publication Data
Names: Lee, Laura (MFA), author.
Title: A history of scars : a memoir / Laura Lee.
Description: First Atria Paperback edition. | New York : Atria Paperback, 2021.
Identifiers: LCCN 2020007955 (print) | LCCN 2020007956 (ebook) |
ISBN 9781982127282 (paperback) | ISBN 9781982127299 (ebook)
Subjects: LCSH: Lee, Laura (MFA)—Mental health. | Psychic trauma—
Patients—United States—Biography.
Classification: LCC RC552.T7 L44 2021 (print) | LCC RC552.T7 (ebook) |
DDC 362.19685/210092 [B]--dc23
LC record available at https://lccn.loc.gov/2020007955
LC ebook record available at https://lccn.loc.gov/2020007956

ISBN 978-1-9821-2728-2
ISBN 978-1-9821-2729-9 (ebook)

For my mother

CONTENTS

A HISTORY OF SCARS

As a rock climber, I'm used to accumulating scars. They're gathered on climbing expeditions, in moments of carelessness or due to freak acts of nature. As someone who bruises easily, who isn't overly precious with my body, I've often not regretted these tangible reminders of the past. They make for good stories, good memories.

One reminds me of the can of beans that exploded over a campfire in Joshua Tree, leaving me with a bean-shaped scar on my forearm from an errant legume that flew through the air and stuck to me like a pebble of hot glue. Luckily we'd bought one of those perforated cans, with a lid designed to be pulled off, so that the lid's flight into the air was graceful rather than chaotic. I associate that bean mark with my oldest sister—I remember how panicked she was by the sound of metal exploding, and how fatigued we were, to not have anticipated the can's explosion. I remember a bulky man with a wiry beard from the next campsite, calling over to ensure we were okay.

Another reminds me of my ex-girlfriend accidentally lowering me from a climb into a large tree, so that a sharp branch dragged across my waist and punctured the skin over my left oblique. The T-shirt I wore dulled the spear-like protrusion's edge, protecting me from worse damage. Another reminds me of limestone crumbling beneath my right foot when I was tied in and climbing seventy or eighty feet in the air, my inner knee grazing a jagged ledge on my fall, an asteroid tail being torn on that soft flesh. The crumbling rock rained down yet spared my ex's head, as she belayed me from below.

I have many small scars. I'm usually sad when they fade, because so, too, do the associated memories—of times when things could've been worse, of moments shared with loved ones, of times when I scraped by relatively whole and okay. Each climbing-related scar transports me to a particular setting, a particular day, a memory where I'd happily dwell.

Then, too, I have a series of interconnected scars that are different. These scars prompt questions that I don't want to answer, and I can't hide them. Not from those I love or hope to love, anyway. They're set in such a way that they require increasing levels of intimacy to witness, so that only those closest to me will see them all.

The fourth of these, purplish red on the left side of my ass, is the worst. Nearly the size of my extended hand, it looks like a particularly vicious bruise, as though I've been whacked hard by something rectangular and large, though nearly six months have passed since my exposed fall onto I-65. I can still see imprints of gravel rubble from initial impact. The third looks like a large set of wings in the middle of my back, from where I skidded down the highway. The left side looks like Africa. The second is above my left hip, but passes as a lightly shaded bruise. The first is on my left elbow—darkly outlined, triangle-shaped, similar in size and shape to a guitar pick; I often forget it's there.

Aside from nurses and doctors, until recently only one person has seen all four—a good friend who unflinchingly bore witness, who asked question after question and listened to my answers, whose brother coincidentally cycled through new, and then repeated, drug-induced psychotic episodes at the same time that I recovered from my hopefully solitary episode, during which these bruise-like scars were inflicted.

There are the official terms, the medical language I'm still learning to use, in the questions I ask myself in moving forward. How soon after involuntary hospitalization, for example, after a diagnosis of PTSD, after a psychotic episode, after a suicide attempt, is too soon to start seeking out human companionship again? How long after the doctors have signed off on your return to sanity can you vouch for your own ability to be a good partner to someone else?

These are the questions I found myself asking in confronting my body. It isn't just in a romantic setting where stigma matters, of course, and where one's own sense of shame polices—where doubts rear up, of whether and how people will treat you differently, once they know certain aspects of your recent past. But it's only in a dating context that my scars are fully visible, would matter to another person—not for their appearance alone, but for the stories they tell. It's in the romantic arena where it feels as though the other person involved has the most stakes, the most right to claim judgment.

*　　*　　*

As with my mother's early-onset Alzheimer's, as with my oldest sister's rare form of cancer (and its timing, accompanied by another cancer), a psychotic episode was something of which I knew little when it occurred, something of which later I had to educate myself. The episode was, as a psychotic episode is, a departure from reality—something that fit outside of the narrative I'd been building for myself, and of my conception of who I was. It meant consequences that surfaced long after the fact, each of which emerged as a shock, which still cloud my way forward. It meant costs great and small, in all forms.

I'd spent a year moving on from the first woman I ever loved. I'd started to put the pieces of myself together, felt hopeful about the future. And then this interruption—another one of the rare medical emergencies with which my family seemed to be cursed. My psychotic episode involved a suicide attempt. It meant my body was scarred, for the foreseeable future.

In reading Yiyun Li's memoir about her suicide attempts, or Esmé Wang's essays about her schizoaffective-disorder-caused psychotic episodes, I saw that both narratives existed in the framework of those settled into relationships—writers who'd already found their people, the partners who accepted their unique selves. In recovering from my own spell in a psychiatric ward, I turned to writers I already knew, for guidance and solace.

What, I wondered, do you do when you're single, and you haven't yet met that person or established that foundation, when your journey in medical realms has potentially only just begun? How long is an acceptable amount of time before you can trust yourself to be whole, before you can trust others to see the value you might have to offer? Before you can say, *I can be good for you, we can be stronger and happier together*, and believe it?

You don't have to tell me, she said. *It's okay.*

I can tell you don't want to talk about it, she added.

But the weight of it still settled between us—the questions that hovered. I could already imagine the ways in which one question might lead to the next, and the next.

I figured you'd see them, eventually, I told her. I was surprised she hadn't seen either of my large scars the first time we'd tumbled into bed together—had been both grateful for the cover of dark, and regretful that I couldn't see the strong outlines of her face more clearly.

If you want, you can just see them both now. I didn't want to hide from her, in the moonlight or at dawn—to think about twisting the back of my body and scooting away when standing up from her bed, which lay on the floor, or pulling on underwear quickly, not for modesty's sake, but to hide.

Eventually she looked at the large scar on my back. *It just looks so painful.* I told her the one on my ass was far worse— which it is. But I also hoped she would simply look at it, so I could know whether the sight of it would break whatever we had between us. So I wouldn't see her shock, in an unexpected moment of revelation. *No. I don't think I want to see that pain,* she told me. *Not if it's worse.*

From that accounting, the scars felt insignificant to me, not representative of physical pain so much as emotional scars. In the time I spent in the psychiatric ward, I routinely refused to let others near the wounds, because I was so fearful of letting strangers approach me. The abrasion on my ass seeped yellow liquid, sticking to the yoga pants my sister had brought me, weeping through the nylon, and yet physical pain registered barely at all. It hurt to sit on, of course, but in a dull way. It still hurts to press. The blooming stains on my blue hospital scrubs surprised me, in the first few days—I didn't fully grasp where they came from, how bad my fall had been, because I was too preoccupied by the fears in my mind.

The physical pain began registering again gradually as I recovered, as adrenaline stopped pumping through my system. One nurse gave me the wrong sort of bandage to apply, despite my request for the nonstick variety, so I found myself peeling off the gridded gauze that had begun melding with my exposed skin. That hurt a little. Over time I began accepting help, and I remember one kind nurse using a pipette to first clean the wound, as I lay propped up on my stomach, commenting that gravel was still stuck in the abrasion a week after the fact, before carefully taping nonstick pads over it. *You probably would've punched me if I'd tried to do this when you came in*, she said with a smile. *Okay, not really—but you wouldn't have let me help.*

The morning after the first time we slept together, she'd already asked me about the scar on my elbow. After a shared breakfast burrito and tall stack of dessert pancakes drizzled in white chocolate and salted caramel, we went to the gym, happy, yet too stuffed with food to climb well.

What's that from? she asked, as we stood next to each other, her on belay, me ready to climb. I didn't know, at first, what she meant, had forgotten the scar was even visible. She gestured to my elbow and repeated, *How'd you get that?*

An accident. A fall, I told her.

Climbing?

No.

I left it at that, but I knew the question had already been raised—not from brevity, but from body language. Our communication style thrived on the unspoken, on sensed emotional undercurrents.

When later in bed, her fingers stroking my back, she felt something on my skin and asked what it was, she felt me tighten up, too. That tension louder than if I'd simply answered. At some point one's unwillingness to share information becomes a bigger obstacle than the information itself. Yet evasion feels easier.

It's from the same thing as the scar on my elbow, I told her.

How long ago?

Six months, I answered. I realized later the inaccuracy of my estimate. Six months hadn't yet passed.

When dating, one doesn't really like talking openly about trauma—it's not sexy. I fell back on that as my excuse. She and I had talked of trauma before, of her unwillingness to read sad stories with unhappy endings or discuss trauma at length, versus my habit of dwelling in and writing trauma narratives. Her desire for silence allowed for reprieve.

Still, my friend saw the feelings I was developing, and she advised me to share specifics sooner rather than later. *You don't want to trap her as your girlfriend*, she told me.

That verb choice, *trap*, did so much work in confirming my fears. My friend had already admitted that she did, in fact, view me differently after learning of my episode, that she worried about my perceived emotional fragility. I didn't want those I entered into relationships with to feel that same burden of caution, in relating to me.

I knew she cared about the present tense of a relationship, not one's previous mistakes. *I don't hold people's pasts against them*, she'd told me. Yet I'd long held the opposite philosophy— that the past and present are intertwined, that one can only truly know a person by understanding the environments they once occupied, and the influences that shaped them.

Perhaps I felt this way because I'd always been surrounded by illness, mental and neurodegenerative and physical ailments, in those I loved. Given my diagnosis of PTSD, I wondered if, without the damages absorbed in childhood, I would have had a breakdown in the first place. I knew all too well the unintended harm caused to bystanders, and the unintended damage caused by silence on such topics.

Even as I, too, wanted my life to return to what it once was, I'd been surprised at how quickly the world expects one to move on. I was familiar with this phenomenon as a bystander to my oldest sister's recovery from multiple cancers. I was familiar with the idea that just as emotional recovery was becoming possible—once finished with treatment, once entering remission—was when one's support network typically fell away.

Yet it still surprised me, to be back in charge, teaching a new class, steering the metaphorical ship, when only eight weeks earlier, I hadn't been trusted to wear pants where the elastic hadn't been snipped out, or use full-length pens to write, or step outdoors, or have the yellow "fall risk" bracelet removed from my wrist, or skip the fifth group therapy session of the day, or possess a watch, even a strapless one, or, or.

One day I received an email from a student, thanking me for making class so much fun that he looked forward to attending each day. On the same day I received a statement of review from my car insurance stating "Diagnostic code: T14.91, Description: suicide attempt" alongside the breakdown of drug tests, brain scans, panels, and assays completed. These documents serve as an interruption, a reminder of severity. You'd like to move on, but six months later, you're still getting those documents in the mail, just when you think you've finally finished with the paperwork and closed that chapter of your life.

These things all coexist. And yet. When you've reached the point of no longer caring if you live, of willfully throwing yourself in harm's way, it takes a minute to recalibrate to the idea of forward motion. To remember that life doesn't stop on a highway, but instead rolls on. Time's passage feels both short and long. How, within six months, does life change from one thing—utterly desperate and out of control—to calm?

*   *   *

The idea of having yet another aspect of my identity which I will continually have to "out" myself on and explain, as with my queerness, or when discussing family with those who assume that everyone springs from a happy, healthy, nuclear family, exhausts me. It exhausts me to realize that I will have to disclose and await reactions from every serious lover in my future, rather against my will, teetering in doubt and uncertainty as to whether the truth behind my scars is enough to make others walk away.

Certainly it will become easier over time. Still, questions of how to handle such disclosures arise. Do you treat future lovers like the infamous frog, where you slowly turn up the heat until they're too relaxed to jump out of the pot? Or, as with an ice bath, do you just shock the system and dump all the details at once? And if so, when? On the second date, by the fourth? Before sleeping together? After being exclusive, but before having official partner status? When is fair to both people involved?

The first time I saw her cooking, breakfast omelets and potatoes outdoors, we were camping in Jackson Falls. She joked about the photos I took of her, as unfortunate proof that she did indeed know how to cook, despite her preference for eating the cooking of others and then, in turn, taking them out to restaurants. What I noticed was not the act of cooking, but the way she held her paring knife: the way she bunched up herbs and pinched vegetables in her palm, then exposed the sharp end of the knife and used her forefinger and thumb to guide the blade's path. It's a practiced motion—if one slips, the knife enters directly into the fleshy part of one's thumb. It's the Asian way of cutting vegetables. Seeing her cutting that way, and hearing her say, *it's faster this way*, reminded me of my mother. My mother had that skill, too—of peeling an apple more smoothly and quickly with a paring knife than with a vegetable peeler. It's a skill I don't possess.

You're so polite, she told me, as we got into bed together for the first time. *It's positively un-American.* In case I couldn't read her tone, she added on, *That's a compliment. It's a good thing.*

When I first saw her, I hadn't realized that she was Pakistani, two years removed from Pakistan, not Pakistani-American. As someone who grew up being mistaken for a non-American, I would rarely make such an assumption about another person. Yet I could feel how much we had in common, in terms of cultural upbringing, by virtue of both being Asian, whether South Asian or Korean-American. I had the odd certainty, upon first meeting her, that we would remain in each other's life in some capacity, regardless of whether in a romantic context, and part of that instantaneous connection involved shared cultural inheritance.

In dating a bisexual brown girl, I shared more demographically than I had with any previous partner. I'd gotten used to the rhythm of being the sole person of color in a relationship—of going along with mainstream white assumptions, of whiteness being held up as the goal, of being the more culturally conservative one, of having to adapt my ways of communicating and moving through the world to fit in with whiteness, of absorbing fault, of translating my upbringing for a white American audience. After more than a decade of dating white men and women, it was a relief.

In being with a South Asian, we had certain instantaneous understandings about family, or privacy, or even how to share food or fight over restaurant bills. Still, a new set of differences arose. I hadn't been the more liberal party in a relationship in over a decade, since the last time I dated an Asian—grappling with religion's effects on the other party then, or in this case, an upbringing rooted in another culture entirely. I tried to grasp a different cultural terrain than that to which I was accustomed: what complications might arise in dating as a bisexual Muslim from Pakistan, where Islam is state-mandated, where queerness is illegal, where no couples, straight or queer, hold hands or kiss in public.

It just isn't done, she told me, about holding hands or kissing, when we unofficially ironed out our codes of conduct for public affection. These discussions are perhaps the usual dance of any couple, and especially any queer couple, in navigating public versus private identities. Beyond just queerness, though, I wondered how growing up in a more culturally conservative country might affect one's definition of legitimate trauma, and one's outlook and attitude toward mental illness.

When I confronted my father about his physical violence, he responded defiantly, *It wasn't that bad*. Which seems, to me, a consistent theme of how one defines trauma. Who gets to say what bad is, what constitutes true trauma? My father hinted often at the turmoil of South Korea during his childhood, during the Korean War, but he never rooted me in the sorts of specifics that would have re-enacted these ideas. He stayed silent.

He stayed silent to protect me, I believe now, from the damaged parts of himself that he recognized. Yet the unintended consequence was that he remained a stranger to me. I knew he had been marked by trauma and neglect, and yet he never provided enough insight for his personhood to be known and understood, despite the obvious ways in which he lived with its effects. Had he given himself permission to recognize the harm caused by traumas inflicted upon him, I doubt he would have been as likely to inflict traumas on his wife and children, in turn.

When I think of traditional Asian culture, I think of my father's values—his refusal to name mental illness, for example, when my middle sister struggled with depressive episodes and dropped out of college, time after time, or routinely dropped jobs. He preferred to avoid grappling with concepts that he failed to believe in or understand. His sense of shame seemed too strong. My middle sister, who confessed to being relieved when she finally accepted her disability, suffered because of that silence, that refusal to acknowledge, to name.

I'm wary of reducing someone to the cultural context from which they come, of their country of origin. Such reductions rely on generalizations and hypotheses, rather than recognizing individuals in all their uniqueness. Yet context matters, in terms of our starting points, in relating to trauma and mental illness and silence.

As I've never traveled to Pakistan, so much of what she says seems steeped to me in being raised in a different country, a South Asian one, with a different values system. I recognize the overlap from my parents.

I understand her desire not to burden her parents with her bisexuality, in the same way that I fear burdening her with my encounter with mental illness. Not only because I fear how I might be seen but also because it's knowledge that she would have to absorb and manage, because it falls outside of our assumptions of the norm.

In the United States, discussion of coming out seems to center on the individual—being one's authentic self, living more happily without secrets. We blame parents and family members who can't accept truth, faulting them as less evolved. In other places, like Pakistan, bisexuality is not something that can openly exist. Why, then, burden one's parents with knowledge they will never be able to accept, that can't exist within the fabric of society as it stands? I understand this argument intellectually, even as I also disagree with it.

Yet I, too, am not out to my parents. Not out of shame, but because I can't see the point of making the effort with my father, when I've shielded every aspect of myself from his view, when we have no real relationship. I can't imagine how my mother would have responded, were she not in end-stage Alzheimer's. My instinct is to assume she would've lacked the language to understand.

* * *

She told me, when we first met, that she had no real trauma—an absolute which immediately drew my attention, because who, really, hasn't suffered trauma, in some form?

Weeks later, as we sat with her roommate sipping green tea and mocha and a chai latte, she calmly mentioned being set up from the moment she flagged transport, being trapped in a rickshaw by motorcycles, being held at gunpoint and robbed, being touched against her will. *It's common*, she said. *It happens. Of course I didn't tell anyone what happened*, she said, not even her family, even as she herself suffered from PTSD afterward.

This silence, I understood, was her act of protection toward those whom she loved, who wouldn't have been able to do anything with the knowledge after the fact, anyway. I understand this attitude—why share information, when it will make the recipient of such news feel helpless? Even as I also believe the stifling of such information causes its own damage, not just to the individual but to loved ones, as well.

This way of handling things isn't far afield from my parents and their ways—not discussing or validating trauma, but burying it, instead. But aren't we, as humans, informed by the process of feeling pain and healing, time and again? Isn't that scar tissue where our true stories lie, where our characters are built? Don't we block opportunities for connection, by denying that most human experience, of being vulnerable, of feeling pain?

I rebel against the stifling of trauma—the desire to silence it—yet I also contain that instinct within me. There are so few people with whom I feel safe in discussing trauma. As with queerness, that feeling of safety only generally comes after the other party admits to their own encounters with such things, only after they make it clear that I am safe from judgment. Or after I've done the same.

When I mentioned to her casually, in our first conversations, that I didn't really subscribe to labels, but that I used queer, bi, pan, I remember she agreed on labels' limitations, but also mentioned that *in Pakistan, no one talks openly of such things*, and so she liked claiming bisexual as a result. Because the question arises of why silence and shame are needed. Ideally, queerness wouldn't need to be hid. Ideally, trauma and mental illness wouldn't need to be silenced.

Yet how do you explain to a Pakistani who views honor killings as a legitimate source of concern, who, understandably, characterizes American feminist concerns as trifling in comparison, that emotional fears can sometimes feel more damning than physical pain?

The emotional pain of having my mind split open was the worst pain I've ever known, even if it was invisible. Don't those who self-harm already know this, that sometimes physical scarring is simply an emblem of what already exists internally, without expression?

Sometimes it takes something as drastic as a suicide attempt for those close to you to recognize the real aftereffects of cumulative emotional trauma.

Still, how do I explain that the scars on my body resulted from my mind turning on itself? I'm used to the disdain that people from developing countries have for our American language of trauma. I inherited it from my parents. As my friend said, recognition of psychological trauma and mental illness is *one of the only areas where we, as a country, are ahead.* Still, here, too, as a culture we seem to only honor pain if it's physical, if it's visible.

When I think of the pains that have truly wounded me, I remember sitting alone as a child in a hospital, waiting for the results of my mother's brain scans, knowing that I was functioning as a surrogate adult, knowing I had no adults I could reach out to for help. I think of my childlike, ill mother, and I remember feeling afraid and isolated.

I often think, with a solid, loving family, with solid footing and tethering to this earth, we can bear anything. But perhaps I only think that because of my sense of its lack.

We rarely intend to inflict the traumas we do. That's what makes them, in some form, forgivable—their accidental, somehow inevitable nature.

In the psychiatric ward, I talked to another patient covered in scars, all over his arms, neck, and face. In my paranoid state, where everyone in the ward was an actor, I didn't believe the cuts were real, that he had caused them. They looked drawn on, like a gaudy Halloween costume. I stared at them inappropriately, surely causing him discomfort.

Another patient kept asking me, in circular fashion, "You're so pretty. Will you be my girlfriend? On the outside? Why not?

But will you be my girlfriend? On the outside? You're so pretty."
She didn't stop following me, asking the same questions on a
loop. An unfortunate coincidence, given my initial fears that
angry queers were after me. She was released many days before
I was.

I often ponder what one can hide—for some of us, one's sexuality, for example—and what one can't. Emotional damage, you
can hide. Still, I have a theory that those who've been abused
can nearly always recognize others who've been abused, because somehow it does manifest itself in visible ways. It's similar
to queerness—if you so desire, you can try to hide your own
queerness; straight people will likely fail to detect it. Other
queers on the lookout will probably guess, regardless.

The scars, you can't hide. The scars raise questions. Worse
when you can't even see them yourself, because of where they're
placed on your body, but others can.

When I sit laughing with her, joking about silly and insignificant things, I can't imagine sharing details of my hospitalization. The beginnings of a relationship feel so innocent and
fresh—one hopes to protect that innocence from harsh realities,
like confrontations with death, without misleading a person.
Those memories feel a world away.

Yet intellectually, I wonder what is accomplished by hiding. I
wonder if, and why, these particular details matter. We all have
our own traumas, but certain ones, society seems to fear discussing. We joke about suicide, but we don't discuss its realities.

The more important questions seem to be, can I guarantee

that I can be a stable partner, or a stable person? Can any of us guarantee this? That we will remain healthy, in body and mind? Can we tell others that it's safe for them to care for us? Can we guarantee that we won't harm them? Or is the universal truth that we will, in fact, hurt those we care about, and be hurt by them, regardless of the specific circumstances?

At what point do you disclose and say, *It's out of my hands, think of me what you will, scars and all*? At what point do you say, *See me nakedly, and decide what you will*?

2

THE BODY, THE MIND

At seventy-two years old, my father still plays tennis with thirty-year-olds, still rehydrates with beer afterward. When I think of him in his most natural state, I imagine the dull green of the tennis court, him glaring into the sun, face stern. Filmy sweat darkening his blue cotton shirt, almost from shoulders to navel, salt stains setting in, and him darting effortlessly across the court, his movement uninhibited.

His face and body can be characterized by juts and hollows—sharp cheekbones, knobby knees, accompanying concavities. He is wiry and strong. He once clocked in at 3 percent body fat on a scale. Beneath his shirt lies a washboard six-pack. His forearms, his calves, are ropey; each muscle individuated.

All those hours in the sun have given him a farmer's tan. My mother used to tease him about his dark skin. As elsewhere, in Korea, skin tone connotes class. Unlike my mother's pale visage, my father's exterior reflects a life lived outdoors.

The twin peaks of athletics and academia are constants in my father's life. His career, as a professor at a small private university on the outskirts of Seoul, centered on engineering and computer science. Yet his bookshelves are filled with books ranging from philosophy to theoretical math manuals to the latest Mary Karr, written in Korean or German or English. It's all interchangeable, as though George Eliot and Leibniz somehow speak to each other. This, in tongues I can't begin to understand. I envy him his mind. I hope, too, for his longevity—his health and vibrancy.

I understand this divide of interests, because my own life is following in parallel tracks, in which the world of the body and the world of the mind are of equal importance. And yet they're held separate from each other.

In a fiction workshop, writers always push for the scene. *Where were you? What happened? Place us*, they urge. I, too, give this advice. When I think of my father, of our interactions, I think mostly of the phone.

He is in an apartment I have never seen, in South Korea. I am in an apartment he has never seen, in Manhattan or Queens. One of us is in my mother's home in Colorado, in a quiet cul-de-sac. One of us is elsewhere. Our paths are elliptical—we avoid each other, even in those brief moments when we occupy the same structure.

When I called my father, from Queens to Colorado, to let him know I was going to graduate school, his first question was, "For what?"

"I'm getting an MFA—a master's in fine arts—in creative writing. In fiction," I told him. I was nearly thirty. We hadn't spoken in years, and though in the interim it had become part of my identity, he didn't know that I wrote. But he responded knowledgeably, anyway.

"Oh, Marilynne Robinson. She teaches somewhere—the University of Iowa. I just picked up *Lila*."

This response startled me. I had only learned about MFAs once I began writing in earnest; in many ways, they strike me as a distinctly American concept. And I hadn't gotten around to reading any of Marilynne Robinson's books. I knew my father was well read, but the degree to which he is still surprises me. It would shame many a writer.

"What school?" he asked. And a minute later, "Oh, that's a good school."

He knew it by its reputation for engineering, I assumed. He had studied physics—nuclear fusion—in graduate school. His reaction to my undergraduate education had been different. He liked to collect my sisters' university mugs—UC Berkeley, Columbia, Princeton. And that of his own alma mater, the University of Illinois Urbana-Champaign, too, sat on his desk. When I brought him a translucent mug encrusted with NYU's seal, he asked, "What am I going to do with this?" and gave it back to me.

A few minutes later, we hung up. But not before he offered to pay tuition. His one steadfast offer, throughout my and my sisters' lives, has been his desire to pay for our education. He sounded relieved when I told him it was fully funded.

"Oh, that's good. That's good," he said. After a pause, he clarified. "It's not the money that matters, though that's good.

It means that you're competitive. To be able to teach afterward, you need to have been competitive enough."

Despite myself, I was pleased. I'd been on scholarship at NYU; I'd graduated in three years. Still, for reasons unclear but palpable, I knew he hadn't viewed that university, that choice, as anything but failure. I heard the difference in tone now, perhaps due simply to lowered expectations for my future. I had accomplished something that he recognized as worthy, even if it was as simple as returning to my education.

That conversation with my father is the most pleasant one I can recall. In our estrangement, I had pushed aside my awareness that the world I was re-entering was a world he knew intimately. Still, there was some relief in that connection. For just a moment, we could understand each other.

When I was about ten years old my father left Colorado for Korea, at nearly the same time as my mother's descent into Alzheimer's began. Now, after his retirement, my father has returned and taken up the mantle of caretaker. This is odd to me, because of my memories of the former him.

Some memories are seared into one's consciousness. Fear does that. It took decades for the nightmares to stop. Even now, when I don't block out thoughts of home, they return, as vividly as though I'd never left.

The father I first knew was the angry one. That man dragged my mother from my bed where she hid, to their shared bedroom next door. He seized her by three limbs, all at once, while the other dangled. I will never forget her helplessness—the way she knew that no matter how she resisted, she was lost. I watched as she slid down the sheets, away from me. I watched as he pulled her down the hall as one might a laundry bag.

She screamed in Korean, but those details I remember less. I lack that language, and so what I heard instead was her fear, and hurt, and vulnerability. Those emotions have their own pitch.

I've tried, as much as possible, to block out these kinds of memories. Yet they don't fade.

I remember him beating my middle sister, three years older than me. There, he had her by the wrist, downstairs, again in the night. It was always at night. Always for some small perceived wrong, some perceived slight: my sister staying up and reading or watching TV rather than going to bed, most often. The screams are what I remember most. Though she was taller and heavier than him, even as a twelve- or thirteen-year-old, or however old she was at the time, fear rendered her unable to resist.

In these instances, I can see the exact setting—the backdrop, the furniture, the cast of characters. I prefer not to. I remember the viciousness of his strokes, wooden, metal-reinforced ruler in hand. I remember his face, nearly animal in its contortions.

That he derived pleasure from hurting someone else, I have never been able to forgive. The forcefulness of his motions has always been linked, in my mind, to his forehand, which he used to practice in the air, sans racquet, over and over and over again, in my parents' upstairs bedroom.

In the single short, stilted conversation I've had with my sister in the time since, she mentioned the bruises.

I remember running outside of the house, into the cool air of my cul-de-sac, on these sorts of occasions. My sister's screams were high-pitched, those of an animal in distress. I could still hear the screams, outside, standing at the edge of the driveway. I can still hear them now. Colorado air is thin—there is little to disrupt sound's transmission. We lived in a quiet, middle-class neighborhood. I wondered why no one helped.

I hovered in the garage once, the morning after a particularly vicious incident. My mother opened the door. "You know what happened last night," she said to me. "Be nice to your sister," and then shut the door.

For a length of time, I resented my mother for absenting herself from any responsibility to protect us. I resented her for sleeping with me at night. I wanted to be left un-pestered, to be granted privacy. My small body functioned as a shield, or a reprieve. I myself didn't seem to matter. She seemed to assume that if she were in my bed, he wouldn't cross that line—he would leave her alone. I found her presence invasive. But I understood, too, that she was afraid for herself.

These are not moments I want to inhabit. Yet I can't remove them from the narrative, as my father would prefer. These are moments that break the narrative.

In the first few weeks of each semester, I teach my students Chimamanda Ngozi Adichie's TED Talk, "The Danger of a Single Story." And yet as I harp on about the value of not reducing a person to one single story, I realize how hard that is to put into practice. Our minds want continuity.

Our visions of those closest to us are so shaped by the impact they've had on our lives, and so inseparable from that, that even if they themselves are paradoxical in their complexity, it's easier to reduce. Especially in relation to certain subjects, like abuse.

Still, it's the disruption of the pattern that can be so distracting. How does one capture a fair picture of a person, if the pieces don't add up to what we expect? Yet it can be tormenting to try to occupy that gray space—in feeling and acknowledging so many contradictory things, all at once, and not knowing what to do with the pieces.

My father tried to protect those around him from whatever traumas he had undergone—suffering the sudden loss of his father as a child, growing up in poverty, as a result, during the Korean War—by not speaking of his past. This is what I assume, anyway. He didn't allow himself to be known. Yet the effects were still clear. He became the trauma. Because of him, normal life seems too mundane—too lacking in adrenaline.

Over the years, I've confronted my father about the past. My family's chronology, geographies, and medical histories are too complicated to plot on a single line. Time blurs. What doesn't fade are his responses.

My father has tried telling me that it wasn't as bad as I remember; that his outbursts didn't happen that often, that memory is fallible.

He has tried to discredit me to myself. To tell me I am an unreliable narrator. His arguments change rapidly, in the style of someone who has a great deal to gain in denying.

He has told me other things, as well, that rather than serving his defense, disturb me more.

I remember where we were standing in the living room of my childhood home, in the most frank conversation he and I have had about the past. It is the only instance in which he has owned up and expressed regret.

With regard to my sister, he argued, "It wasn't just one-way, you know. She hit me, too."

When I responded angrily that she was a child, that she was trying to defend herself, he fell silent.

With regard to my mother, his defense was similar; that it wasn't just him, that she escalated.

"Even if that's true, it wasn't an equal fight," I told him. "You're stronger than her. She's smaller than you. What kind of man hits a woman?"

To which he said sadly, "How was I supposed to know better?"

I asked him how someone so intelligent, so well read, could have had such a complete lack of respect for women.

His response was that their fights were actually a sign of respect, because it showed that he viewed himself and my mother as equals. He added, too, "I wouldn't hit her now. Because she's not equal anymore. You see?"

That sentiment was supposed to make me feel better, I think—to reassure me that he wouldn't hit a woman suffering from mid- to late-stage Alzheimer's. He wasn't that sort of man. Yet to this day, I find that comment the most disturbing. That logic can be so twisted.

In that same conversation, I challenged my father to fight

me, as an adult—to try to hurt me. "If you want to hurt someone, fight someone who can fight back!"

Even at the time, I could see how warped my challenge was. How it was issued long after relevancy. Yet somehow I needed to proclaim it—both to let him know that I wasn't cowed by him any longer, and to finally stand up. To rid myself of my fear of him.

His response was sadness and confusion. "There's something wrong with us. I thought you were different. She always said you were nice. But you're so angry."

I demanded to know whether he regretted anything he'd done, whether he was sorry.

"Yes, of course, I'm sorry. But what can I do now? It's in the past."

He'd never been able to admit to that before: regret. Somehow, after all the denials, the counterattacks, the refusals to engage, it was the only thing left unsaid.

He and I rarely saw each other. He hadn't known, until that conversation, how much those memories tormented me, and how much time I spent trying to understand this man, in spite of myself.

His advice to me, too, was "Forget about it. You should just move on with your life."

That conversation felt final. After that, there was nothing left to say.

Like my father, I can't go back in time. I can't alter my narrative. I can only write into the future. It wasn't that my father was blameless in his outbursts, in those moments late at night, when

I would hear him rushing down the hallway, or down the stairs. I knew the warning signs for his explosions.

But what has haunted me since, in my nightmares, is my helplessness. The way I simply let things unfold, as though I were watching TV. I watched, and did nothing, as the ones I loved screamed for help.

When my mother became violent in turn, the most I ever did was hide rulers. I knew what she meant when she asked me angrily once, "Where is it?" I stowed the wooden ones I could find in my closet and told her I didn't know. The next morning, she threw away white plastic fragments, shatters from the flimsy imitation she'd used against my sister, instead. Those wooden rulers, oddly enough, are still at home today.

In the single conversation in which my middle sister spoke of the bruises my father inflicted, she told me that my mother's violence was the one she couldn't forgive—because though my father was much stronger, he was a stranger to her. It was my mother's betrayal that hurt. My sister has told me, too, how much she hated me; for many reasons, but in part because I was left untouched. He left before it was my turn.

I've never fully forgiven myself, for the way I bore silent witness, without realizing I could have acted. In some ways I was just like my mother. I did nothing to stop the violence, partially because I was afraid for myself.

In the interim I've built myself up, physically and emotionally, to protect myself from people like my father. And people like my sister, who became so aggressively violent and angry, in turn, that even he was afraid of her. I've also torn myself down—to make physical, and exterior, the inward pain.

I bought a punching bag, hung it in the basement, and learned to fight. I learned to protect myself not from my father, but from my middle sister. I remember, still, the last time she attacked me. It was the only time I fought back. She stopped after that, because she knew that I was stronger than she.

I lifted five days a week. I bench-pressed and leg-pressed multiples of my body weight, 125 percent or 150 percent or 300 percent, depending on the exercise. I tested my pain threshold, pushing myself so hard that it hurt to move each day. It made me feel strong.

At times it feels difficult, to find the balance. To project enough strength to signal to those who might hurt me that I can defend myself, without driving away the ones who wouldn't want to in the first place. In some odd reversal, the difficulty has become learning to be vulnerable. To let in the love of those who can still see the person I once was, before I erected walls.

I've thought back, often, to why I felt so frozen in inaction. Even when I was a child, less than ten years old, I had a sense of foreboding. I understood the consequences. I imagined my father in jail, losing his job, being deported. His citizen status was uncertain—I knew he was a permanent resident, even if I didn't know what, exactly, that meant.

Looking back, I don't know that the ten-year-old me could have done things differently. I sensed that my mother wanted our lives to remain private—that she distrusted Americans, distrusted institutions. I imagined, too, my mother bearing the burden of young children and a job, alone—a burden that she eventually bore, regardless.

I remember my oldest sister, home on a visit from college, while he was also visiting on a break, threatening to call the police if he didn't stop. I remember him shouting back at her, "Go ahead!" And I remember her doing nothing.

There were moments when I dreamed of someone else calling the police, of my father realizing consequences. There were moments when I dreamed of doing it myself. But I didn't do anything.

It took me almost thirty years to call 911. Even then, I did so only after asking my neighbor directly.

"Do you want me to call the police?" I asked, as she stood a few feet from me, blood streaming down her face. "Are you sure?"

That fear of getting involved stops many of us, I think, even as adults, even in moments of crisis. We don't want to interfere. Even when people scream for help, it can be easier to pretend not to hear.

At some point, we have to do something. It wasn't till I was almost thirty that I did something. It didn't cure the problem— life isn't that simple. But it did mean that for at least that night, the punches stopped. Maybe, for just that moment, that was enough.

And in that sense, it was so easy. I wondered why it had taken me so much to take action, even when I'd seen the other side of it, even when I knew how quickly violence could escalate.

Though we judge those in abusive relationships for not getting out, we also don't intercede on their behalf, to help. Because on some level, we also know how messy it is—that things aren't that simple. And so instead we turn away.

In the years since those childhood flashes of violence and anger, I've somehow hit middle age. Even as I only now am learning to stop seeking the seat closest to the exit, to stop planning my escape route.

The moments that have given me peace have been both large and small. Some of it has required matching that intensity of fear with equal intensity of happiness, of love, from sources able to give it. To grapple with me, in safer ways.

Part of it has come from finding my own natural home—in refuging for the past fifteen years on the cliffs, as a rock climber. In embracing a lifestyle equally intense in its sensations of fear and joy. In which I choose the risk I'm willing to undertake. In which I can choose my own way. In which I choose not to flee, but to endure.

Part of it has come in having started to forgive myself. In having, for at least one moment, protected another, as I'd once wished to be protected. Part of it has come in knowing that I can protect myself, and part of it has come in finding people who I know will protect me. Who take my version of the past as what it is: my truth. Who will not invalidate it, because they are not benefited by a false retelling.

Part of it has come in seeing what a different man my father is in his actions now, in caretaking. Part of it has come from recognizing that his and my lack of relationship arises now out of mutual recognition—that we will never be able to communicate, that we can only cause harm to each other—rather than out of a place of anger. Now, it is freeing, to know that my father's opinions hold no sway over my life or decisions. I lived in his shadow. It is only through disregard that I have emerged.

Biology fascinates me. Think of rats birthing in trash bags on crowded streets in Chinatown, on Mulberry Street, feeding on scraps of dim sum, or mosquitos releasing rafts of spawn into still puddles of rainwater. This is r-selection—rapid reproduction, in which having many offspring compensates for a lower likelihood of each surviving and reaching maturity. Then think of the converse, in creatures that nurture: giraffes, elephants, whales. This is K-selection, in which more investment is made in fewer offspring, instead of the more scattershot approach seen above. Humans, too, are supposed to fall in this second category.

I've often thought of r/K selection theory in relation to my own family, and families like mine. Without the parental investment typical of K-selection creatures, what becomes of these long-lived offspring? Do we find our own way, or do we succumb to the same forces that felled our parents? Do we become lost? Are our lives as valuable as those who were nurtured, in conventional ways, or are we forever stunted?

It isn't just about r/K selection theory, either. It's also about our most fundamental images of nature, the ones we see on all the nature documentaries. We see a predator—coyote, hyena, lion—approaching a cluster of sheep or gazelles or zebras. We see the herd breaking into a trot, gazelles springing in every direction, but still swarming in one trend. And then eventually we see those who lag, slowly but noticeably falling behind. We know it's one of these creatures who will be felled, one of these sick or elderly or simply not as sure-footed. How does it feel when you know you're one of those falling behind, wondering if the lion is going to spring on you, savage you?

Then, too, there's genetics. Those who write fictional versions of Alzheimer's disease rarely pay heed to the personality changes it involves, beyond simple memory problems, to the unpredictability of the day-to-day. My sisters and I used to fight over genetic testing. We, who grew up with the chaos of our mother's degeneration, wanted to know if that same clock was ticking in us.

My oldest sister didn't want to know, couldn't bear the concept of that information being available. Because genetic testing for early-onset Alzheimer's would've begun with mapping the APP, PS1, PS2, and APOE4 genes in my mother's blood, not ours, because Alzheimer's has no cure, because genetic testing requires counseling, it isn't possible to get testing, as far as I know, without the consent of all affected by the results.

My family inheritance seemed a late November apple, riddled with worms. Our history lost, our bloodline tainted with illness. Then, too, beyond simple genetics, there's the environment of family. My father and middle sister taught me about the importance of self-protection. It was due to them I learned to wrap my fists in tape, put up a punching bag, and defend myself. I tried to learn how to unfeel the pain of my own blood. I began lifting multiples of my own body weight, and later in life I began rock climbing, as a physical reprieve from all the ways in which I was powerless.

We climbers talk of base strength. It's one's base strength that matters, as much as one's upper body. Your vertical grip begins with the curl of your toes, which travels up from your base to your knees, hips, core, and then finally your forearms and fingertips.

When you toss your body upward, lunging for a hold, and fall, screaming, twenty or thirty feet below, the fault lies, more often than not, in the tilt of your toes against the edged rock: the angle, the push away of your center of gravity. It's just physics.

Your ability isn't measured in how many party-trick, fingertip pull-ups you can muster on doorframes. It's measured in balance, knowing how to shift your weight over your toes; timing, when to throw for a hold; and power, flexed biceps unleashed as last resort, lactic acid pumping through veined forearms.

It's in how thoroughly you've caulked the cracks of your body, jammed white putty in the crumbling red brick of your fears. I can cross-train the rotator cuffs of my shoulder girdles. I can arc-weld the metal of my mind. I can send those fuckin' badass climbs, the ones that bisect the sky.

But what if my odds of inheritance are already imprinted on my genes? What if patches of steel wool can't keep mice from swarming? What if the only thing I can do is climb into the sun, hoping I've built enough base strength to carry through?

Whether I want there to be or not, there are similarities between him, this stranger whom I've never known, and me. I used to fight it—to dismiss any parts of myself that resembled him. To want to reject every part of him, which meant rejecting large chunks of myself, as well. Yet, though he and I may have superficial interests in common, I can see now that we are also innately different from one another. I own that knowledge.

It has taken this long, for me to learn to let go.

I've lived a life full of my own mistakes and adventures. Yet throughout, my actual outward journey, the one I tell myself when casting my own story, has been one related to family. How to reconcile myself to its fractures, how to heal myself. To do so, I've had to put as much physical and emotional distance between us as possible. I have strived for normalcy.

Even now, at thirty-three years old, a few hours near my father's energy are enough to threaten everything I've claimed for myself. It is hard for happiness to take root near someone so deeply dissatisfied, so deeply angry. He is so deeply damaged and unforgiving of what has harmed him, in a way that I recognize, in a way that I hope to dispel from my own character, in my own time.

I know that I will never feel safe near my father.

He is someone whom I will never be able to access, whose entire life will pass me by, just as mine has passed his, our stories brushing up against each other only occasionally.

3

ALUMINUM'S EROSIONS

After a recent climbing trip to Jackson Falls, in rural Illinois, I sorted through old gear in my apartment. I wanted to collect bail biners—the carabiners that allow a lead climber to bail off a pitch before reaching the route's anchors, without forfeiting more expensive gear.

As a teenager foraying into lead climbing for the first time, I blundered and made mistakes. As an adult, I'd accumulated wisdom and experience. It felt, in a tiny way, part of the great equilibrium of the universe.

But life is never that linear. A climb that straightforward would be uninteresting—a climb's unexpected detours and features are what make it worthwhile.

After years in an MFA creative writing program, climbing only sporadically and experiencing a number of personal setbacks, I'd lost my confidence and my ability. I hadn't led outside in nearly nine months. I didn't have a guidebook to the area, and so I eyeballed a route that looked like a warm-up from the ground, but climbed several grades harder than expected in the air. I like strenuous, upper-body-intensive routes—this one required precise oppositional body positioning, balanced on the downslopes of bulges, reaching for damp holds I couldn't find. It required, more importantly, mental strength, of which I had no reserve.

My girlfriend tried the climb, made it a clip higher than I did, and then I took another turn before deciding I didn't have the nerves to take multiple falls while working out the moves—and so I lowered off a biner I'd retrieved years ago from glowing white, pocketed limestone in Wild Iris, Wyoming.

I remembered the man who'd left it behind. I was leading seventy-five feet of endurance, power, and flow, a classic for the area. A few body lengths below me he worked the neighboring route. His wife belayed him, as their child played nearby. We had chatted before we began. Twenty- to thirty-mile winds buffeted us, but that only added to the convivial spirit of the day. Their child spoke in a mixture of Spanish and English, tiny plastic toys spread in the dirt around her, and so we mimicked that. "Un pájaro," my ex-girlfriend said playfully, after finding a bird that had disappeared from sight, tucked away in a naturally formed nook.

His fingers were bleeding onto the sharp pocketed holds—later I could see the stains from above, had heard his commentary as he pulled regardless. Because his route was less trafficked, rock crumbled and rained near his wife and child. Neither wore helmets, and so he did the smart thing and bailed.

On my way down I reached over and snatched the biner. Usually bail biners are a shiny prize you spot from the ground and collect on your way up, or something you stumble across. This was the only one I'd cleaned on the way down from a route, rather than picking up more "legitimately." Usually they're impossible to return to the original owner. I would've handed it back, but the threesome had already retreated to whichever campsite they'd staked for themselves, blending into the landscape around us, filled with blooming purple wild irises. They'd said their goodbyes before disappearing around the corner.

Instead I strung this otherwise unremarkable biner— unpolished silver in color, D in shape—alongside others I'd picked up in different geographies, in Oregon or California, Wyoming or Thailand, each with its own backstory.

On that day in Jackson Falls I didn't regret quitting—I knew the climb would be waiting for another day, when I understood the area's style better, after I'd warmed up. I did regret losing this particular biner. I struggle to part ways with old gear. A brand-new one would've been generic, unbranded. This I associated with good memories. Memory is funny that way—it imprints itself on whatever's at hand, whatever's convenient.

In sorting old gear, I came across my old set of quickdraws— two carabiners connected by a dogbone, or stitch-reinforced nylon sling. I'd used this set for nearly a decade before retiring them. Nylon degrades from UV exposure and abrasion. Metal itself wears thin. First the coating wears down, the purple varnish or orange paint, and the gloss of aluminum shines through. Then the aluminum itself erodes. I understand the aging process, but this wear on metal is what amazes me the most. It's not insignificant.

Friction from rubbing against climbing rope does its work, and grit and grime help the process along. On my most worn draws I can see a thick groove on the bottom carabiner's elbow, developed because this is the snug spot that cradles the rope. I can rest my finger in the concavity formed.

Notching my finger there feels a testament to something—to what, I'm not sure. To the passage of time, I suppose. To the repeated exertion that's left its tangible mark on the sturdiness of metal.

When these concavities get deep enough, sharp enough, they can slice through rope, in an alarmingly clean fashion. Rope is strong in terms of weight-bearing load, but it isn't resistant to knife-like edges. Despite that, these grooves amaze me more than they disturb.

I tend to be safety conscious. I follow manufacturer recommendations even if gear is visibly fine. I played around with an old dogbone that I'd never used, one that looked new, and the rubber meant to anchor a bottom biner in place snapped and fell off in my hand. A good reminder that age and deterioration aren't always visible, that gear needs to be abandoned periodically, preferably before it's too late.

Fifteen years have passed since I first started climbing. I can track so much of time passing through the rock, even if the chronology is blurred. The timeline is peppered with the sorts of traumatic events that have kept me running away, for most of my life, until another pops up, and then I swerve in another direction.

It's peppered, too, with a flood of happy images. This has something to do with why I can't part with old gear. Climbing has been a lifeline, tethering me to this earth. It's been my way of retreating from failures and events beyond my control, to lick my wounds. Of testing what a romantic relationship is made of. It's inflicted pain, bruises, injuries, loss, and it's also healed. It has been the only activity the intensity of which matches the intensity of fear I've experienced elsewhere. The difference with climbing is the intensity of joy it also contains.

These other images have recurred at different points in my life. It was really over a decade ago that I struggled with what felt like PTSD: persistent flashbacks of moments in which I was helpless, nightmares that haunted. But I grew up with my parents' distrust of doctors, suffered the consequences of doctors failing to diagnose my mother with early-onset Alzheimer's for over a decade. I grew up with their distrust of institutions, of systems, of neighbors, of "Americans," of people, frankly.

Rather than seeking help, my climbing obsession began— its timing a happy coincidence. I put minimal effort into my schoolwork, spent all my energy instead reveling in the intense body-feel of climbing, the physical act of problem solving, the challenge.

Climbing has been the constant. It's where I can occupy the best parts of myself, and battle with my worst. There are injuries, there are years I barely climb at all. But whenever I return, I feel free again, temporarily free from burdens. I can battle and fail, and if I walk away safe, laughing with my climbing partner, then it's been a good day.

I didn't seek help until my thirties, didn't receive a PTSD diagnosis until after I'd suffered a breakdown. The terms, the labels, the diagnosis helped me understand what was happening to me. But climbing is what has given me space to be. Climbing is my own.

Gearheads talk about how the new coatings or the new carabiners themselves aren't built as they used to be—of how the carabiners wear down more easily than in the glory days of yore. I don't know if that's true—although I've had some biners inexplicably wear themselves down much faster, right from the get-go. It's comforting, though, to think that things used to be different, before.

I read recently about how we experience time differently as we age—how we compress experience, so that decades pass in a blur, where once a year was an eternity. The same happens with climbing—there's a time when every lead fall means something, every improvement, every new texture and angle of rock, and then there's a time when it all blends together, becomes as normal a part of life as routine coffee is in the morning, or the act of reading the paper.

I read, too, about how trauma exists outside of linear time, outside of language, and this, too, feels true. Over the years I've read findings from psychology, from neuroscience, from writers and artists, always following this same repetitive path, in hopes of finding a way to construct meaning for myself out of a life that hasn't made much narrative sense. The biggest relief I find now is reinforcement that when fracturing occurs, there is no continuity. We just make it up to comfort ourselves.

*　　*　　*

If you're a certain kind of person, you can feel others' pain exquisitely, and your own, but you lack the ability to vocalize it. You find other ways of expressing it.

"Can she talk?" a private music teacher my mother had hired asked, on our first meeting. I was, from a young age, wordless. The pain I'd frequently felt was that of observation—of witnessing others' traumas, suffering from their bad behaviors, and of feeling powerless to do anything about it. I didn't just feel that way—I was powerless. I was young.

To speak requires trust—that someone will listen. It was easier, then and now, to be silent instead. To be a jock. The one who lifted weights until it hurt to move, while men nearby stared, who ran until I landed in a walking boot.

Even now that I can speak, silenced by each new inexplicable event, there's so little meaning there. Each trauma suffered has pushed me back into that silence. They've felt endless, relentless. The cumulative weight has, at times, felt too much. It has broken me—physically, emotionally.

Climbing can be hard to explain to the uninitiated, hard to visualize: the ways in which rock is bolted every few body lengths with metal hangers, into which a leader clips the top biner of a quickdraw, into the bottom biner of which the leader clips the rope that is their functional lifeline. Below stands the belayer, or the climbing partner who feeds out rope through a belay device, watches for potential hazards, catches falls, and eventually lowers the leader back down to the ground. Of course there are variations: traditional, multi-pitch, aid climbing, bouldering. This is only the language of sport climbing.

More than the mechanics, though, it's the psychology of climbing that's always fascinated me. The ways in which how someone climbs reveals much of their character, and the ways in which it reveals our more primal instincts relating to fear, trust, risk, and consequence.

"What do you think we all have in common?" a fellow climber asked me once, someone I met camping, after she eyed the canned corn I was dumping into my pasta and offered to share some item she had, in exchange for some yellow kernels.

I spent the next afternoon climbing with her and her husband. They, like me, were living on the road, sleeping in the back of a minivan, climbing full-time. They, unlike me, were deeply religious, had the innocent glow of a young couple in love. I envied the support they had in each other, that they thrived jointly off of this dirtbag lifestyle. "Why do you think we do it?"

I didn't answer her then, as was my wont—to stay invisible through silence, even though that silence only meant that people would project what they wanted on me. I couldn't say with certainty—but my gut instinct was that every serious climber I'd met was acting out something that was beyond words, grappling with past traumas or demons. Or perhaps they were just built for a different time, when adrenaline and physicality mattered in a way that contemporary society doesn't reward.

This seems a question many of us grapple with, though. Why we're different in this particular way, in this particular obsession. Another old climbing partner, a strong one, told me, "I wish I didn't have to climb. I don't like getting dirty. But I have to do it."

What compels us to continue in an activity that involves endless amounts of failure, not an insignificant amount of pain, and scrapes and scars and injuries and all the rest? I know only that it makes me feel more present, more alive. And yes, happy, in a way that feels earned.

Just as traumas don't make for polite dinner conversation, they don't fit neatly into stories or narratives. But we have to escape somewhere, to grapple with them. For me nature was the answer. Had been since I was a kid. I grew up having seen my father's faith in nature as a restorative. I spent little time with him in general, but those times involved camping near some national park, hiking some mountain.

As a dirtbagger I marveled at the amount of wasted potential there was, in my fellow dirtbaggers and myself. Strong dirtbaggers are problem solvers primarily, with a high threshold for pain and discomfort. I've often marveled at how that energy might be channeled if redirected, even as so many of us want nothing more, perhaps, than to be left alone.

Rather than process or cope, you can fill your head, instead, with all the minutiae that living a dirtbag lifestyle on the road entails. Where meals, rest stops, bathrooms need to be preplanned or figured out on the fly. Where training can be scaffolded. Where what might be junk mail in another setting becomes instead fire starter, or something else equally useful. Where dives can be discovered, adventures had. Where one can disappear from real-world troubles in favor of being off the map, in favor of the next pitch of rock. The meaning lies in what the pursuer can excavate, in self-discovery, in friendship, in healing. It's not just the climbing that matters, obviously. It's everything else.

I remember talking with someone once long ago, someone famous in climbing circles for the pizza shop he owns, which serves as a basecamp of sorts for that region's crags. Like the dirtbaggers I remember from over a decade ago, the shop seems to have had an evolution of its own, seems to have matured to a different state of being. The shop's façade and clientele has changed greatly over time, as its popularity has exploded in lockstep with climbing's popularity, but its soul seems aged rather than altered.

I remember him telling me, about the seemingly driftless dirtbaggers that lived, for $3 a night, in the campground he'd established behind his shop, "They come back in a year, and they're scientists, engineers, back in school."

He knew his shop functioned as a rest and recuperation spot for certain lost souls. He knew I was one of those lost souls. He knew the dirtbag lifestyle is, for most of us, temporary. That some needed reprieve, as we ran away or figured out our next steps.

He gave me a fat white winter radish to eat once, as he commented on the spicy mustard greens I'd gotten on discount. Not being from the South, I hadn't known how aptly mustard greens were named. It was one of those small acts of kindness, of humanity, that made a difference.

*   *   *

There've been very few times when I've been numb to the fear of taking a lead fall. I remember sitting next to my oldest sister as red doxorubicin dripped into her blown-out veins. To fight the cold of the drugs, she draped over her the soft furry white blanket I'd gotten her, and on the tiny screen of her chair of that fancy Manhattan chemo ward, we watched the Williams sisters play at the U.S. Open. I remember going to the climbing gym during those months and feeling absolutely nothing as I took big lead falls. Climbing felt unimportant, irrelevant.

Then there've been times, too, when I've been numb to everything else, and the fear rush of a scary climb has let me feel joy and pain and emotion again, rather than dislocating from myself. When I sort through climbing-related images, they don't all make sense. So many injuries. So many sends (or successfully completed climbs, sans falls). They flood back with no sort of logic or chronology about them. The act of climbing mirrors trauma. The intensity matches the images I sought to flee.

Here in the Midwest I first objected to, and then resigned myself to, all the labels by which we're meant to identify. These labels have, in Trump's America, become part of the national conversation. I could say I'm bisexual, queer, Korean-American, a person of color, fill in the blank with the terms of our time. Terms which I use now only because they're a way in which I can be understood, because they're true, and for the sake of others' comfort.

But none of those labels get to the heart of me. I can love a man, woman, nonbinary person, white person, brown person, black person, Asian person, American, not-American, whatever. Doesn't matter. But I've never had a serious relationship with a non-climber. It's too essential a part of me.

There is no single narrative, for anyone or anything. The only narrative through lines I've been able to find in my work, and in my life, have been climbing and those I've loved, because everything else seems fragmented, distorted. Trauma does that—renders life meaningless, unwhole.

Trauma memoirs thrive on the acting out. I re-enacted my trauma mostly through choosing a sport intense enough to mirror the past. Climbing grapples with life and death honestly, at least. Visibly. Climbing is what I chose.

As a writer I see trauma can't be captured in isolation—it can be measured only in images, quantified only in its aftereffects. When you've grown up with a mother who has suffered from nearly every symptom of each of the seven stages of Alzheimer's while remaining undiagnosed, who was often delusional throughout your upbringing, it's hard to know what reality should look like. When you've suffered the abuses of family, it's hard to know what decency and kindness are. When you are this silent, you become a mirror to others, partners and strangers alike.

There isn't a clear "before" and "after"—there's an "again" and "again" and "again," only each time different, new. It exhausts slowly, a war of attrition. It was long-lasting, started young, and it eroded my sense of self. It's not easily understandable, because the images don't come as clearly.

"In some ways it was worse," my therapist said to me about the kinds of trauma I had experienced versus the kinds of physical violations that are often more validated or legitimized, discussed or understood. I'd needed the sorts of trauma I'd experienced to be legitimized, to be observed. "It wasn't a one-time incident, but something that recurred."

I began seeing her only after it all became too much. "Entered first lesbian relationship, broke up with girlfriend in past two weeks, grieving her ex-girlfriend's father's death in a climbing accident in days after," the intake notes say.

Ideally conversations about trauma shouldn't begin and end in questions of blame, or in comparison of degree. What they should reflect is consequence: that deeply felt trauma leads to real, long-lasting consequences that shape one's future. That these consequences affect those around us. That they require time and effort to heal, and they do not simply fade on their own.

Finding ways to come to terms with trauma, and to heal, isn't selfish—it's essential. Both to self-preservation, and to finding a way to move through the world without causing harm, to oneself or others.

The problem with re-enacting trauma, as a form of salvation, is that salvation always has the power to destroy, too. To devastate. The stakes of climbing are truly life-and-death, even if gyms will minimize them to the language of a liability waiver, even if the activity has become mainstream. I doubt there are any climbers who've been at it for a few decades who haven't known someone personally who's been paralyzed or lost their life.

When I think of my ex-girlfriend's father's death, I don't think of the moment itself. The enormity is too much to grasp. I can conjure no mental image of his fall, the full half mile of it, nor do I want to. The images I do have, of the aftermath, I try to block out. Instead I picture happy images from our last trip together. I picture his daughter's grief.

The only comfort might be in that he knew the risks. He chose. That is the great appeal of climbing. Unless one's partner is at fault, the wound is self-inflicted. These wounds can be equally senseless, equally difficult to live with, but at least there's no wonder about why someone else chose to do what they did—why they could be so unknowingly cruel.

With a certain type of innocent climber, I wonder, sometimes, if they're aware of the possible consequences of their new fitness routine. If the potential for loss feels real to them yet.

You can't manipulate the end result in climbing, without improving yourself in technical terms, in mental strength, in physicality. There's some sort of fairness that doesn't necessarily exist in socially constructed systems. Sometimes you don't get the second chance.

We carry with us the memories of those gone. On a different day, that harsh logic of gravity might've cost another of us. We might have made a tiny mistake, committed a small act of forgetting.

* * *

I finished sorting through my old gear, deciding what to keep and what to discard. I know that Jackson Falls bail biner will be there, waiting for me, unless someone has snatched it up before I return. If it's gone, I'll wonder whether its new owner will remember the contours of that climb, or that day. Whether they'll palm it as a memento. Whether it'll later appear on a different crag in a different state, for another climber to collect.

4

SEASONAL DENIAL

For much of my life, I lived in denial of seasons. As a child dressing for soccer practice in Colorado, for example, I didn't learn how to prepare properly for wintertime weather. I donned my short-sleeve jersey, shorts, shin guards, long socks, and cleats, even when I was stomping through thick shoals of snow. I was the only one on the field dressed so ill-preparedly, my exposed skin reddened. Despite the freeze, I acted as though I didn't feel the frigid air, going somewhat numb to it instead.

As an adult in New York City, I established my habit of walking down sidewalks carefully, of hopping around large puddles at intersections where water pooled, rather than buying rain boots for torrential spring rains. Sometimes that meant taking a running leap, or glancing over my shoulder for blue Citi Bikes and cyclists before stepping out onto black asphalt. I got used to landing, in any commute, in a wet splash, my socks soggy and cold, when distracted by cabs, people, or my own thoughts. Inevitably I suffered some lapse in every journey, where I'd forget to be careful. But somehow this system of mine seemed more logical than investing in plastic boots, which would only be worn for a few days each year, and which weren't something I'd ever learned were an essential. My motto was not to live or dress seasonally, but to live and dress the same in every season, defiantly and without reason. I forgot the seasons were going to change, until the switch was thrust upon me.

I only changed my behavior when I moved to the Midwest, where seasonality doesn't allow itself to be ignored in quite the same way. Where gloves are a necessity, where I own a car for the first time, where door locks freeze themselves shut, where I've learned about winter vehicle maintenance, about warming the engine and scraping down the windshield in the mornings and evenings.

This sense of denial seems a family-born trait. Members of my family refuse to recognize the truth of our circumstances, until we're absolutely forced to. This trait is beyond the comprehension of outsiders to my family, who ask, "But how could you not have known?"

The greatest source of friction over denial within my family has been in my relationship with my oldest sister, ten years older than me. In fairness to her, she applies this principle to her own life, as well, if unwittingly. I saw this principle in action in the hours after her first chemo treatment. I was twenty-five to her thirty-five, at the time. "I want to go for a long run," she told me, after we made our way in a cab from the Upper East Side to her apartment. "Before it's too late."

She was genuinely ready to strap on her running shoes and hit the pavement for an eight- to ten-mile run, not yet ready to think of herself as someone who was ill, in the present tense, not ready to think of her beloved running routine being taken from her. I was concerned about the basics—whether she needed her prescriptions for anti-nausea medication filled, whether she was stocked up on the things I'd read about being helpful, like ginger ale. She had different concerns.

"Maybe you should just lie down," I tried to convince her. Within the hour the chemo had kicked in and she was passed out on her sofa, while I snuck out to Duane Reade.

Her and my relationship has defied easy categorization, over the years. She remembers me as a baby. "You cried so much," she used to tell me, with fond irritation. We became friends only when I was in college, when I began inviting my sisters to the climbing gym at which I worked, when we began frequenting bubble tea and frozen ice parlors near my college campus downtown, where she often treated me to large concoctions, covered in mango syrup and mochi and tapioca pearls.

She and I grew up in different geographical states, and in different eras of my family. When she was growing up, my mother received assistance from food banks, at times, visited dental schools to get work done. My parents were still finishing their PhDs and beginning their teaching careers, at times living in different states.

When I grew up my mother was financially successful, upwardly mobile as a tenured professor, and, in flush, happier times, she was preoccupied with things like upgrading most of the flooring in our house from carpet to hardwood and tile. My parents were living and working in different countries.

My sister was away for college, then graduate school, then work, while I was still living at home with my mother as a child and teenager. She called home often, visited home on breaks. My mother, in particular, seemed a different person during the short visits my oldest sister made home when I was growing up. She gossiped with my oldest sister as she would a friend, her personality changed, hiding the worries that consumed her when left alone with what were, in comparison, children: my middle sister and me.

Over the years my parents each individually responded to my oldest sister as a plant responds to sustenance, their tendrils visibly firming up, drawing water through their veins, and rotating their upturned faces toward the sun.

Still, there were signs of my mother's decline. My mother grew increasingly concerned with financial matters when I was a teenager, obsessive beyond reason. One day she panicked over the size of her credit card bills. She'd given my oldest sister permission to use that card in graduate school, but now she worried about the figures coming in—the restaurant dinners and other amounts beyond her control. As she kept complaining to me about the situation, I called up my sister, shrilly voiced my mother's concerns.

"Fine, I'll stop using the card," my oldest sister told me, irritated, before hanging up.

When I was a teenager and my sisters were together, they used to play a game with me. Any time I would start speaking, one of them would cut me off. I would begin again, and the other of them would interrupt. I would keep trying to pick up the pieces of my story, and each time I did, another interruption would come, until finally I became so upset I was on the verge of tears. For some reason only I was susceptible to this game—I became visibly upset by being denied my voice, and that I could be so upset was what encouraged them to keep playing it. By the time they both relented, I no longer remembered what I'd meant to say in the first place.

My sisters and I used to play other games when we were gathered together, too. We crowded around our giant PC, to play the CD version of *Jeopardy!*, in which we would each pick a different computer key to buzz in and then type our answers. We played Scrabble, which, in our literary family, was held in higher regard than more arbitrary games like Monopoly or Life.

I remember the first time I won Scrabble, because I didn't just win once—we played all night, my oldest sister determined to set things right by winning a game. We'd hung up a giant whiteboard above the wet-bar banister that divided our living room, and on it we tracked words in red and orange, words that had been challenged before being located in the dictionary. We stayed up, and I kept winning, time after time, proving my first win wasn't a fluke. I'd proven my own mastery over vocabulary, over language. I'd won. Something had changed. I don't remember ever playing again with my sisters, after that night.

I learned early that verbalization, the ability to speak, meant running up against someone else's narrative. I came from a family in which one person winning meant another person losing. Within my family my voice always seemed to represent a threat.

*　　*　　*

In college, I spoke with my mother over the phone, much as my sister had done a decade earlier. My mother repeated the same question, over and over again: "When are you coming home?"

"I can't come home, I'm in college," I told her, before hanging up and drinking shots of cheap vodka from plastic jugs, as a release from the pressure valve of guilt and angst she unleashed in me, as a form of self-punishment. My mother's only interest in these phone calls seemed to be hounding me about this question, implying my failure via absence. By "come home," she didn't mean come home to visit. She meant come home to live for good, and to take care of her, as she often told me.

In these phone calls, my mother told me other things, too, things that disturbed me because they simply weren't true. Once she told me she remembered visiting the rock wall at which I worked. "It's pyramid-shaped," she told me. In another call she told me about how I'd been studying and living abroad in Prague, when I'd never been to the Czech Republic. In another call she'd decided I'd become engaged to the person I was dating at the time, which I decidedly hadn't.

In reality I'd flown to college alone, with two suitcases' worth of clothes, and she'd never visited me. The rock wall I worked at wasn't pyramid-shaped, but flat. I'd signed up to study abroad in Spain, but because of the paperwork involved, I hadn't been able to.

It was the particularity of her imaginings that both confused me and provided her with certainty. She was so convinced of the validity of her ideas, of her reality, she often made me doubt myself, as we debated back and forth whether her firmly held beliefs were true. I tried to convey the troublesome quality of these calls to my friends, but they didn't understand why I became so upset. "So your mother thinks you got engaged when you didn't," a friend said. "Just tell her you didn't, what's the big deal?"

In isolation, perhaps any one instance of confusion might have seemed innocent. It was the sheer accumulation of tiny things that disturbed me. I tried, more importantly, to communicate my concerns to my oldest sister, whom I appealed to for assistance.

Because my mother herself had for so long feared getting Alzheimer's, this disease was the one I'd long wondered if my mother was developing. Whenever I broached the subject, though, my oldest sister said, as though the statement were final, "But she's too young." She often delivered this verdict in her apartment, in the presence of her boyfriend at the time, who had a PhD in biology, and who concurred with her opinion.

Trying to sway her opinion felt a task insurmountable. She didn't want to hear about my mother's worrying behaviors. I'd given examples, but individually, my sister dismissed each one as explainable, as minor. In the presence of her skepticism, I failed to verbalize. I hadn't enumerated all the many behaviors I'd seen from my mother that alarmed me. They were too numerous and too exhausting to catalogue, partially because I had only vague ideas of what normal behavior from a mother might look like. Presenting such behaviors to an unwilling audience held little appeal, particularly when I was only beginning to sort out the mess of my childhood.

My mother had been diagnosed, at some point, with a mild cognitive impairment, and my oldest sister was unwilling to believe anything more serious was wrong. I witnessed more than I was capable of enunciating. Had I been able to enunciate it all, it would've been more than my oldest sister would've been capable of hearing. She simply didn't want to hear me, or to entertain ideas that she believed impossible.

My mother was finally diagnosed as I was turning twenty-one, a few months after I had graduated college, and after I had just moved to another continent halfway around the world, with my then partner.

Though I was the youngest, somehow I was the only one able and willing to return home, to take care of my mother. Because my own independent life hadn't yet begun, I returned to file her application for disability and to manage the first of many crises. During that time I appealed to my oldest sister for help with paperwork and tasks, but she didn't respond with any tangible action. She didn't help. She left me alone to deal with caretaking.

There always seemed to be a fundamental disconnect in how my oldest sister and I communicated. I experienced this particularly when it came to expressing things I wanted for myself, independent of my family.

As we sat eating dinner at an Egyptian café in Bangkok, on our trip celebrating her post-chemo recovery, I told her, "I want to be a writer."

She responded, "I think you make a really excellent consultant."

It was a typical response, indicative of the quality of our communications. When I told her I wanted to go to grad school, she wasn't supportive. She told me horror stories instead, about how it was a path to nowhere, with professorship jobs impossible to get. It was never what I had wanted—to be warned of the horrors, rather than supported in what I wanted for myself.

Years later, when I decided I'd done as much for my mother as I was willing to do, I replicated my sister's absence while in graduate school and while working, in favor of going to graduate school myself, and focusing on my studies rather than on making emergency trips home. She angered over this choice, in return.

"I need you to fly home," she told me, to take care of something related to my mother, the weekend before I needed to take the GRE. I knew doing so would throw me off balance, and I wanted, for once, to stay focused on my future.

"I can't," I told her. I'd reached the point where I was no longer willing or able to continue returning home without forewarning, a choice for which I didn't apologize. No one who hadn't been there when I was growing up with my mother had any right to judge. They had no idea what I'd been through.

Her response was to get angry, to berate me for saying no.

My oldest sister and I thought of ourselves as the "healthy" ones, at the time; my middle sister had long absented herself from any family responsibilities. If either my oldest sister or I absented ourselves from caretaking responsibilities, it fell upon the other party to pick up the slack.

"I just feel so alone," she complained bitterly to me, often, a sentiment I knew well from my own upbringing. She, too, had left me alone.

*   *   *

When I am thirty-three and my sister forty-three, we have a long phone conversation, nearly six hours long, in which we discuss our complicated family history. Our mother has just died. I've just been diagnosed with a serious mental illness, one with roots in both genetics and environment.

My oldest sister admits to me, about having been expected, implicitly, by my parents, to pass on lessons they'd passed on to her, to have a hand in taking care of me and my middle sister, "I resented it."

I've always sensed this resentment from her, regardless, don't need her to admit it to me. It comes across in the little things— the way she's kept her social circles hidden from view, the way other transplanted siblings living in the city share apartments or live in the same building, where she has always made clear she wants her geographical distance from us, that she values her independence above all.

Her resentment of this expectation is tied to my sadness over how little of a relationship we had, for most of my formative years. I, too, have my resentments—mainly about the times when I needed her help, and she wasn't there to provide it.

My family, never the happiest, self-destructed in my oldest sister's absence, as my mother grew sick, as my father departed for South Korea, as my middle sister descended into her own undiagnosed condition.

"I'm sorry for the times I was mean," my oldest sister tells me, and then, as an afterthought, "and that I didn't listen."

But it's this, the failure to listen, that has bothered me more than the unkind comments accrued over the years, whose sting I still recall.

Honest conversations about uncomfortable topics have never gone well with my sister. She similarly didn't believe me about my father's violence when I was growing up, until, in my midtwenties, I had emotional backup in the form of my then partner, who stood with me in the yellowing linoleum of the kitchen of my childhood home, as the three of us stood together there, all of us visiting to take care of my mother. She hadn't believed me about my middle sister's abusive behavior, until she witnessed me confronting my middle sister about it after I'd moved to the city for college, when my middle sister didn't deny anything, but instead apologized.

The denial that always stung the most, though, was in relation to my mother. It caused me to doubt my own reality. It had consequences in terms of responsibility; how could responsibility be divvied up for problems unacknowledged?

About my mother's illness, my oldest sister tells me, "I didn't want to believe that was true about someone I loved."

By the time she told me this, after my mother's death, I'd already deduced this logic on my own—that all the times my sister had refused to listen to me had originated from this reflex, both self-protective and protective of my mother.

In the years prior to my mother's diagnosis, my wisdom teeth were impacted. They needed to be broken into tiny pieces and vacuumed out.

You're going to need someone to drive you home. Someone re-

sponsible, said the surgeon. This, due to the general anesthesia I would undergo.

The consent form language of allergic shock, stroke, heart attack, and other risks didn't worry me. This mention of a *responsible adult* did.

Can I take a cab home? I asked.

But he was quite firm.

And so the day of the appointment, I drove to the doctor's office with my mother in tow. She was tasked with taking me home.

I had returned to Colorado only for dental work. My mother had wanted me to stay, to *take care* of her, rather than attending NYU. I wanted nothing more than to leave my childhood home. Everyone else had left, after all—my father, my older sisters. It was my turn to go.

I lay reclined on the chair, dentists and nurses and other personnel clustered around me. One held a mask to my face and counted backward from ten. Probably my last thought, while drifting away, was, *Colorado is so white.*

I woke, groggy and confused, and saw the door of my mother's tan minivan moving closer to my face. I didn't know how I'd gotten there. Then I realized I was sitting in a wheelchair, and one of those white faces—a dental assistant, perhaps—was pushing me through the parking lot.

The last thing I heard, before I was left alone with my mother, was the assistant's instructions: *Don't talk. Keep your mouth closed. Clamp down on the gauze pads so your gums don't bleed excessively. Otherwise you might knock blood clots loose, and you'll end up with dry sockets. Take painkillers.*

Once we were alone in the car, my mother turned to me in the passenger seat and asked, *Where are we going?*

Through thick layers of gauze, I warbled, *not . . . suppose to talk! Hrme!* Then my mother drove off, and I passed out. Still fuzzy from the procedure, I fell back and forth between drugged sleep and wakefulness. Each time I woke, I caught a glimpse of the passing streets and trees and buildings. I wondered why we weren't closer to home, but then I faded out again.

Until those persistent and familiar notes—fear, panic, and despair—in my mother's voice awakened me.

Where are we? Laura, where are we?

It's like a punch line of a joke, isn't it? The Alzheimer's jokes people still insist on telling me, even after they know my mother is dying.

But it isn't funny when you've just had surgery. When your mother hasn't yet been diagnosed with early-onset Alzheimer's (and still won't be, for quite some time). When all you want to do is lie in bed with some codeine, feeling itchy but pleasantly drowsy, and your mother, tasked with returning you home, has absolutely no idea where you are.

The biggest problem in this instance was the disruption to her routine. She had no pattern to fall back on, and so we were lost.

I felt betrayed. I had done so much for her, and yet she couldn't do this simple thing for me. As usual, she needed me to take over. I needed someone who, for just this brief sliver of time, was capable of taking care of me.

I wondered how other *responsible adults*—the ones with the authority to matter—her doctors, my father, my sister—could not see what was so clear to me. My mother was not okay. She was not *too young*.

I made yelling noises through the metallic, blood-soaked gauze in my mouth, gesturing, while she got more upset. *Mmmrph not suppose to talk! ERGH!*

I tried to stay mindful of warnings of dry sockets. But I was angry. We sat side by side, feeling equally helpless and disoriented, for different reasons.

I wondered how those same doctors, and those who say *maybe it's better not to know*, might feel if they knew my mother was driving on the same streets as them, veering slowly—and as unpredictably as amyloid plaque tangles in the brain—across four or five lanes of traffic, relying only on the watchfulness of other drivers to move out of her way.

Nearly every time someone learns that my mother had early-onset Alzheimer's, they try to relate by telling me, "my grandmother/grandfather had Alzheimer's!"

I want to respond by saying the illness is an entirely different beast when it strikes decades earlier. That it's different when it's your mother, when you're young when the decline begins. I want to say that this beast of an illness upends conventional expectations of who will be responsible, who will be the caretaker, and when. But as with my relationship with my sister, there are some truths that are too difficult to discuss. There are some truths that are too hard to hear.

*　*　*

Over the decades my oldest sister's and my relationship has endured, despite periods of not speaking, alternating with periods of pointless fights. We have supported each other over the years, in the worst of times. Our relationship has been shaped by emergencies—each of our responses serving as pivot points on a graph. Perhaps the forge of family blood is unique in how it weathers such rifts. But as with sawn wood, look closely and the grain is always visible.

5

WRITING LIFE

When I was in the hospital, I scribbled away furiously. I felt as though, along with more valuable things like my very sense of identity, writing was being wrested from me, and so I fought harder for its preservation.

I clutched the only pen nurses would allow, a half-stub toy of a thing. Gel-coated and squishy, it made my left hand sore. Still I carried on, scrawling in the two wide-lined notebooks my sister brought me, my handwriting even messier than usual.

Little did I know that my hospital writing, under the auspice of its fuzzy panda and fuzzy fox covers, would contain more logic than any of what followed. Little did I know that after I left, empty months would follow in which I couldn't write a word.

So many of my fears during my psychotic episode actualized after the fact—around how people portrayed me, their intentions, and their lack of trust.

It'll take me years to unpack how conflict with a person in a position of power, someone whom I should have continued skirting, escalated to the degree it did, or the tremendous consequences that followed.

I was meant to be writing my MFA thesis. Instead I was confronting the hangover effect of my episode. My life had flipped into a nightmare, much as it had during my episode. The larger issues still loom and are hard to discuss. They boil down to how mental health emergencies are viewed in the law, something over which I have no control.

The instigating events rendered the small town I lived in miserable. I avoided triggers—a purposeful strategy, yet no easy feat. A friend tried dodging encounters with her ex in the same town; she essentially couldn't leave her apartment. I clung to Zadie Smith's words on avoiding cliques, gangs, and groups instead—relieved that at least one writer could be both brilliant, successful, and an outspoken critic of the tyranny of the majority.

The larger consequences of my episode unfolded gradually, each fresh blow landing just as I'd recovered from the previous shock.

I arrived at a juncture where I was teetering. My future might involve impossible highs—five years without financial worries, writing at a dream school with dream professors, in a dream city. Or impossible lows—jail. Both extremes originated in the same decision: moving to a place where I knew I'd struggle, in favor of getting a writing education.

I could justify the three increasingly hellish years I'd spent in rural Indiana by finishing my MFA, or I could fall one completed thesis short of a degree. The only thing I could control was my work, and at that I was utterly failing.

"Your essays are lacking a sense of purpose," my thesis advisor told me. With her usual clarity, she hit upon the fundamental issue in my writing, as with my life: that I'd accumulated images and experience, without knowing what to make of any of it. The utterly fracturing experience of a breakdown, in which my very mind felt cleaved in half, hadn't helped.

"You have all the tools," a visiting writer had told me just a few days before. "Now you just have to put it all together."

Cohesion—what I'd always desired and lacked.

There's value, nearly always, in writing through the pain— capturing the images. The notes I wrote in the hospital were surprisingly usable, even if the conditions under which I wrote them were less than ideal. A psychotic episode renders a person overly fixated on the sorts of details that comply with the "show, don't tell" mandate that'd been hammered into my skull. It was the larger picture, seen in a clear frame of mind, zoomed out from the details, which no longer reflected reason.

Imagine a mouse running down a string, parcels of gouda tied at regular lengths. Imagine the mouse's joy. This is what writing technique is meant to accomplish. Even in nonfiction, art isn't meant to mimic life. It earns its power only by distilling these most painful and joyous moments into consumable morsels, all tidily arranged for the reader to discover.

When you're experiencing catastrophe in real time, without the benefit of built-in time for reflection, you're often too busy scrambling to fulfill a core responsibility of a nonfiction writer: generating meaning.

The work of an essayist requires facing up to past trauma, finding meaning in what would've best been sidestepped, unearthing bits of hope. Nonfiction forces you to inhabit your own pain, instead of co-opting someone else's. That's what makes it hard.

One of my most promising students knows the story he wants to tell—he just doesn't share it with us. His language is beautiful, but we're never clear on what's happening.

I share this tendency, in writing and elsewhere—to focus on everything but the most important part. Grief, numbness, and anger do strange, distorting things to a person. So, too, do denial and lack of control over one's circumstances.

My academic training is in fiction, but the form has never fit me comfortably. It's like a typical women's top, cut to different proportions than my own. Climbers are often built like gymnasts— torsos broader at the shoulders, narrower at the hips. This lack of fit doesn't mean our bodies are wrong. It means designers' conceptions of female shape and form are faulty, or too limited to universally apply.

Fiction, as it's taught, demands simplification. In short stories, for example, we're taught a central conflict is meant to emerge. My life experience runs contrary to this idea of one focal point—the prism through which all else is understood. It's this pat quality I reject.

Rather than a prism, I see a wheel. Rotations controlled by forces beyond us dictate extremes. I've been buried by chaos, filth, everything undeservedly rotten, all at once, or conversely, been heaped with equally undeserved blessings. A fallacy of youth seems to be that we generate our own luck.

Defining conflict by one dimension alone, or assigning blame in human interactions and human-made systems—such undertakings are rarely neatly or fairly done. Isolating one variable as a prime driver is fraught with imprecision. This is why economists are accused of dealing in abstractions when they identify exogenous, or acting, forces.

Fiction techniques taught feel restrictive. As with any other product, packed neatly for sale, they're designed with certain dimensions in mind. They don't allow reality, as I know it, to be captured.

I'm complicit in the system, of course. As a teacher I parrot similarly flawed advice—and learn as much as I do as a student in doing so. Disillusionment and reconciliation seem part of maturing as a writer—accepting the measures by which gatekeepers define "good writing," resigning oneself to less radical change than what one once desired. Perhaps women's tops designs don't need to be thrown out entirely. Perhaps they need only to be tailored.

The more exciting aspect of maturing as a writer is disavowing rules entirely. Rachel Cusk in *Outline*, Catherine Lacey in *Nobody Is Ever Missing*, Maggie Nelson in *The Argonauts*, many others—writers I admire break form. Rather than define a good container as one with cylindrical curves or four equal planes on which to rest, they seek the best container for the content. Perhaps oil is suited best by dark glass, to delay rancidity. Perhaps alcohol is best suited to wooden barrels in which it can breathe. Perhaps food scraps are meant to live with maggots in dark bins, until they decompose into something earthy and organic and vital again.

The great surprise of writing has been how much companionship matters. After nights spent alone with my laptop's white glow, it's the resurfacing that revitalizes.

I graduated from my undergrad a year early. I'll be lucky if I finish my MFA months late. If I do, it will be because others extended faith, gifted unexpected compassion. Sometimes we rely on the kind words and encouragement of others to persevere. Not wanting to disappoint those who've extended faith can be a surprisingly excellent motivator. I've experienced such extremes, in the best an MFA has to offer, and the damage it can inflict.

Shortly after I first started climbing, a sponsored climber stopped by the gym where I worked. He brought videos of himself bouldering, brought cans of free Red Bull in a giant Red Bull–shaped cooler.

After his screening, my boss volunteered me to try a dyno problem in front of everyone else, or a move in which the vertical distance between holds is so great that you have to launch your body upward in the air and catch the next. The sponsored climber was meant to help me learn and send this particular problem. He gave vague advice about getting my feet on to start, stood behind me, and watched.

The problem was set on an overhanging prow, so that throwing your body upward also meant throwing backward into negative space. To grab the next hold, you had to aim a few inches above it, so that you could essentially fall and latch on to the jug. I'd tried the move a few times on my own without success—I'd fallen just a few centimeters short.

On my first attempt under his watch, I committed. I threw my body upward and landed the dyno with a satisfying thump.

"I didn't do anything," he said, surprised. By this he meant, I think, that he hadn't touched my back to support the move. He hadn't physically assisted me, and his beta, or advice, had been nonspecific.

This moment has since become familiar to me: one in which success or failure lies with the energy of those surrounding you, rather than in your own mental, physical, and technical abilities or limitations.

He had helped me, simply by giving me a reason to fully commit. I knew him then as a sponsored climber. It was later that I saw him as a regular person, separate from his media persona, someone trying to make a living by selling a certain kind of dream.

Even at that work event, rather than selling adrenaline and success, the stories he told were of the takes we didn't see—when he tried to repeat what he'd already successfully sent, was too tired, and paid the price in broken bones. The sends don't come without associated costs.

In Kentucky I climbed once with a newer climber, someone who was physically stronger and better conditioned, but who didn't have the confidence of experience.

"It's like watching you climb a route in the gym," he said as a compliment, as he watched me warm up on a route.

When it was his turn, I could see hesitation manifest itself in his body. Doubts translate to moving downward rather than upward, to pausing when you should be throwing faster. We yelled, "C'mon!" in these crucial moments, and he kept pushing. He reached the anchors successfully, without falling or asking his belayer to take his weight.

When climbing's hard, it feels very hard. You watch people moving and you can't imagine their elegance, their power. And then when conditions have aligned, you're the one floating up rock, remarking at just how easy it is. At how it feels like we're meant to do this, made for it.

After he lowered he acknowledged that we lent him belief, that he'd surprised himself by sending. I remember him talking about the "good energy, the people," how everything had felt right.

I've been both the one benefiting from good vibes and the cheerleader helping others send. It just depends on relative experience and the moment.

Climbing and writing aren't dissimilar in that the value in both is inherently noncommercial, nonmonetary. In both we do what we need to get by on the expertise we've accumulated, through pain and effort and mistakes. In both it's the act itself that matters—the hours spent working, for the sake of the motion itself.

Sometimes the best beta to get is from someone of similar height and build. Sometimes the only way to persevere is by looking for guidance from those who've already traversed the same paths, who've already battled through crux sequences and found their way to safety.

Both activities are asynchronous to modern society. For all but the rare few, acts like climbing and writing become the medicine that allow us to function, rather than the meat and potatoes on which we subsist. Only the lucky and gifted can sustain themselves on such acts.

The best mentors are the ones who don't need anything—who opt in, regardless. They lend belief when none is in sight, when self-generation of such confidence is difficult to near impossible.

It's clear when mentorship stems from pure motivations. Rather than trying to stake claims to their own greatness through association, these mentors provoke genuine gratitude without demanding such in return. They're givers.

In certain climbing areas, technical ones like Jackson Falls, where sections are blank of holds, moves can feel impossible, until you shift your way of thinking slightly. Once you reconsider your body position, the placement of your feet, what sort of a move you're going for, what you consider a hold, suddenly the move can feel effortless.

Essayists have mainly the material of our own lives to work with. Piecing together shredded narratives can feel like an act of desperation. As we examine our own faults and mistakes, it feels akin to drowning in the pressure to convert carbon to diamonds.

In working an essay I feel the moves out as I would a climb. Hips in, or hips out? Body square to the wall, or body crouched down low? It's the maneuvering that feels good—becoming aware of parts of your body you didn't know existed, or alternatively, parts of your mind and thinking.

You can only climb or write hard when you've put fear and panic at the consequences of failing aside. As you focus instead on discovering what's required to succeed—the small gains rather than the big throws—solutions start emerging.

A typical climbing routine outdoors might be two days on, one day off; two days on, two days off. After a few weeks, climbing can cross from a joyous activity to a monotonous one. Physical and mental exhaustion accumulate. After a few weeks, those rest days can become the real highlight. Writing days are equally grueling. It's the disruption of time away that allows for progress, both in physical exercise, where super-compensation dictates that we become worse before we return stronger, and in writing, where our desires to communicate hop-step beyond our technical skills.

Support from others helps, but writing is fundamentally a solitary task—one both publicly performed and privately practiced. Away from performance and deadline pressure, what reinvigorates is that rediscovery of pleasure for its own sake. No one can take away the hard-earned wisdom of training on one's own, of pushing past doubt. There's no substitute for that feeling. The reward is in finding new pathways, as we expand our visions of possibility.

Just as in climbing, when the foundation isn't strong, the essay isn't going to work. It's obvious when you're flailing, when you're hoping hope will be enough. It rarely is. Similarly when you've set up correctly, when you're going to land the move, you know it.

When soaring, both feel the same. There's the moment, after having accumulated enough technique, after letting go of self-consciousness—when the motion becomes instinct. When no one else's voice matters. When the motion becomes a way of returning to quietness, to oneself.

6

DEPARTURE

The emotion I most strongly associate with my father is anger. And yet when I accompanied him to the local Social Security office in Colorado, what I saw instead was vulnerability. I'd agreed to help him apply for spousal benefits during a brief visit home, years after I'd filed for my mother's benefits, when I was twenty-four or twenty-five. Because my mother received Social Security disability payments due to early-onset Alzheimer's, my father was eligible to receive monthly payments of one-half her benefit amount.

I'd finally convinced him that he should apply for spousal benefits when he mentioned casually that wheat bread was too expensive to buy, and so he had been buying white bread instead.

"I don't like it, but I can't afford wheat," he told me, as we stood in our kitchen, lined with yellow linoleum. "It's two dollars more per loaf." He shook his head.

I preferred only returning to my childhood home when my father was elsewhere, in Korea. On a rare occasion when I visited with a friend, my friend told me my father and I avoided each other whenever we were both within the house, something I hadn't noticed on my own. It was true, though; we followed elliptical paths, attempting to prevent collisions.

Despite our differences, in that moment of discussing bread, I was struck by sadness. Poverty was so entrenched as part of my father's identity. As a family, we could have afforded wheat bread, but he didn't feel he could. He didn't regard my mother's financial resources as shared, especially given her condition. And he himself had accumulated very little in the form of life savings. So he chose to continue downsizing his quality of life, rather than ask for help.

We drove over to our appointment in our family's maroon Honda Civic. Our car was so old and broken that I had tied red ribbon around the windshield wiper lever and secured it with Scotch tape to the steering wheel, to keep it pulled up in its place. Driving required a gentle touch. He insisted on driving.

When hitting bumps in the road, occasionally the lever would jigger loose, and the wiper blades would fly furiously across the windshield until the driver repositioned the lever gently into its notch. Accelerating required physical effort, too, in pushing the resistant pedal down slowly, slowly toward the mat.

Visiting from New York City, where all government offices that I had entered were broken-down, grim affairs, I thought the small office presented the brightest possible picture of local government at work. The square, squat building was efficient, clean, filled with sun, and spacious. There were even happy, smiling employees, to boot.

After checking in with the security guard, we were quickly ushered into the cubicle-lined back-office area. The woman conducting our interview was white, with long brown hair, and of average height. She looked so innocent and fresh. I imagined her to be a newlywed, someone who was passionate about helping others. I remember few other details about her, except that at certain moments throughout the interview, I felt her respond to my father with suspicion.

I had dug up my parents' marriage certificate from the ugly brown cabinet in their bedroom where they kept such things. I had armed myself with a manila folder containing his Social Security card, passports, my mother's tax return, disability application, and other such documents. Even with those forms, the woman kept asking for things we didn't have.

"Can I see a copy of your birth certificate?" she asked.

My father explained that he did not have one, for complicated reasons relating to the Korean War, lack of record keeping in South Korea, and his parents' short-term relocation to China.

This, I could see, confused her. As did the idea that his income statements were written in Korean, because he had lived there for the majority of each year until retirement, and needed to be translated to English. Each question became more taxing, because of the details of his nontraditional American life.

"You've been eligible since your birthday. Why didn't you apply earlier?" she asked.

I had wondered the same thing. I had told my father many times that he should apply, but in typical stubborn style, he had insisted that it might not be a good idea. In his thick, guttural English, he explained haltingly to her that he thought he needed to wait. At the suspicious look on her face, I jumped in to explain that he hadn't known what to do. She seemed suspicious as to whether his vulnerability was an act.

When I'd filed my mother's application for disability, her future had been uncertain. Her application had required doctor involvement, and the approval process was opaque. Failing to receive funds would've been disastrous—she'd already been forced into early retirement, and the funds were acutely needed. She herself was past the point of comprehension, and she needed someone else to intercede on her behalf.

With my father, the barriers to aid were constructed by him. I had told him he would receive one-half benefits; the guidelines were quite clear. But he persisted in fearing that perhaps he might need to wait. He had been eligible since his birthday, but he had been afraid to go.

He had always been this way—somewhat hapless in America. He was wildly intellectual, but he spoke in English with a heavy accent, and he'd never learned to speak in English without a degree of hesitation. This left him unable to be understood by impatient servers at restaurants, unable to call plumbers on his own, unable to manage finances, or complete other normal activities of living.

Of course, his personality played a large role in this learned helplessness, as well. He constructed walls around himself, refusing to ask for help when he needed it. He was suspicious of strangers, distrustful of lawyers, and deeply protective of his privacy.

When salespeople called our home in the evenings, as they often do in suburban settings, my father never learned to react calmly. Instead, he grew agitated. Each time he picked up the handset, the trajectory was familiar. "Hello? Hello? Yes, who is this? Where did you get this number? Why are you calling me? Don't call here again! Do you hear? Don't call again!"

At first he sounded uncertain; by the end he would be screaming. After he hung up on the poor salesperson, he would mutter darkly, frowning. I tried to explain that it wasn't worth getting so angry about; that this was their job, that screaming accomplished nothing. But my father had established his patterns in life. His reaction to any perceived lack of control was a hot temper. In his strongly held sense of personal ethics, the salespeople were clearly encroaching on his rights.

We somehow made it through the woman's questions, and we walked out with a printout, explaining the lump sum he would receive for six months prior, months in which he'd been eligible to receive benefits he hadn't claimed. I remember his smile of relief when we got home. I'd rarely seen him so happy. I understood it as the freedom from worry that financial security offered.

Despite all our differences, our long-entrenched estrangement, for a moment I felt as though we'd endured something together. We'd triumphed, for once. Our relationship was no better than it had been before, but at least he could return to eating whole wheat bread, buying Gruyère cheese in ten-pound slabs from the local wholesale warehouse, and picking up the occasional book from the local bookstore. Those were, and are, his ideas of splurges.

My father and I know next to nothing of each other's life, then and now, but my family has always been tied together by pragmatic concerns—by finances, by illness, by need.

For most of my life, my parents were ciphers. My parents were individuals who had to be understood on their own terms, rather than as a unit. I never learned their origin story, of how they came to be a couple. They confided separately their complaints about each other and their marriage, but not the happier moments. They tended not to speak positively of each other.

From my mother I learned that my father had accidentally landed at the best university in South Korea, due to some administrative chaos caused by the Korean War. This fact grated at my mother, who considered herself much harder working, but who hadn't experienced such luck.

"He's smart," my mother said often, bitterly. She often spoke of him as the smarter one, disregarding her own status as the breadwinner, the one who handled real-life concerns.

As for my father, at a bar where he drank cheap beer and chewed on spicy wings, he told me once, "I should've married someone like your mother's sister, instead." By this he meant he should've married someone without my mother's "temper," as he put it—a comical complaint, given his own instant-flare, white-hot personality.

Only in searching the most mothballed corners of memory do I find any memories of my parents in what could be construed as happier times, or engaging in social activities. I rarely saw them interact with others, never saw them express affection publicly. Strangers were rarely invited into our large, empty suburban house.

On rare occasions when my parents hosted a party, my father retrieved a few dusty Heineken bottles, coated with drips of white wax, from the kitchen pantry where they were housed. He stuck white candlesticks into the green bottles, so the long tapers stuck out at lopsided angles. The cardboard lid of a Domino's pizza box would serve as the backdrop for a board game, on which he drew shapes, and the adults gathered around and played. Small wooden sticks completed the game, or perhaps served to keep score. As with so many other parts of my parents' lives, the games were mysterious.

My mother might fill a metal leaf-shaped tray with nuts and put out a cheese ball, too, the size of a grapefruit. Certain aspects of American entertaining, as with cheese balls, seemed to fascinate her. Other elements of her own upbringing she retained—bringing out orange persimmons or yellow Korean melon or purple seeded Kyoho grapes or mandarin oranges for dessert. It was as though they were playing at entertaining, assembling their own rule book.

There was nothing classy or sophisticated about their gatherings, but the company was a welcome interruption from the seclusion of our lives. Beyond these rare interruptions, other adults almost never appeared in our house. My parents seemed to exist mostly in a vacuum, context-less, as a result, without reference points beyond their interactions with and comments about each other. I wonder still if their isolation was geographically imposed, by virtue of having so few neigh-boring Korean- or Asian-Americans with whom they might share a common background, or whether it was intentional and self-chosen.

When I was a child, before he departed for Korea, my father had short spurts of energy, in which he would playact at being a father figure, trialing out some idea or another on us. He left cooking to my mother. If anything, he brought us to McDon-ald's or Burger King, where he would eat a burger and we would eat fries, but once he took me to the grocery store and lectured me on what I should buy. He told me, "If I give you a dollar, you should buy apples with it, not candy bars."

As another lesson to me, he donated, unbeknownst to me, a cherished stuffed animal that I'd been gifted, a soft and furry and fancy rabbit. When I returned to my room, the stuffed ani-mal had disappeared. The intended lesson had been something about how it's better to give than receive.

In sports, too, he had ideas. We had a battered copy of Steffi Graf's biography lying around in one of the many bookcases in our house, and he encouraged my middle sister and me to read it. Like her, he seemed to want us to be tennis champions. His muse seemed to be Steffi Graf's strict father. He encouraged us to practice forehand and backhand swings in the air, twenty-five to a hundred times each, if possible. When an uncle visited from Korea, he, too, wanted to see our tennis swings. The only problem was that neither my sister nor I liked tennis much at all. Nor were we natural talents.

We lasted for one unwilling stint at tennis day camp, where we practiced our serves, where I tried to even out my toss, throwing the fuzzy ball high above my head, time and again. After that either our lack of talent or our apathy became apparent, and we stopped the tennis experiment. Instead my middle sister and I watched my mother and father on occasions when they played, serving as their ball girls by ducking at the white net midcourt before chasing down balls.

Sports were my father's domain. On this passion he and I overlapped, although we still failed to speak a common language. I preferred playing basketball, a sport in which he tried to instruct me. Never mind that he himself didn't know how to play—he was worse than I at making a basket. When we stood on the downward slope of our driveway, where I'd somehow convinced my parents to install a hoop, his gait was awkward. His knee bends were overexaggerated and ill-coordinated with his upward push, his elbows sticking out sideways at odd angles as he tried to shove the ball toward the net, at a sharp angle rather than an elegant swoosh. He hadn't learned from any coaches himself; his form was terrible. It didn't matter. For a brief period, he accompanied me to basketball games. He couldn't help coaching me post-games, with his tick-list of all the errors he'd seen me make throughout the game. Afterward, until I was left in tears from all the errors he'd point out, he'd say, "You're doing this wrong. You need to do it like this."

Mostly, though, the lessons I learned from my father revolved around isolation—how to exist in wilderness, how to thrive in it. Unlike his other experiments, trips outdoors were a routine aspect of his lifestyle. The mountains beckoned. He'd grown up near them in Korea, always escaping on some adventure. If we weren't headed toward the mountains to hike, we were on a road trip to some national park, to some patch of nature. We went most often to Wyoming, where mosquitos the size of dragonflies congregated on the tarp of our cheap green family tent. We bypassed motels in favor of tents nearly always.

I remember him driving in the late night, clutching the wheel, drinking McDonald's coffee to stay awake, grouped together with other cars, following their taillights. From those trips I remember my father trying, and failing, to start fires with cardboard boxes and empty soda packs. I remember him making chicken soup, made with so many jalapeños that the watery broth choked us and seared our throats. The only ingredients? Chicken breast, water, and jalapeños.

Other memories float through—the odd, empty saloon we stopped in during the day in Wyoming, crowned with animals' heads on the walls. A man having a heart attack on a hike in Devils Tower national monument, his wife calling for help, my sister and father running back toward the visitor center.

I remember the lectures, as we rounded hairpin turns snaking up craggy mountains. I suffered motion sickness from the whiplash effect of our car swinging from one side to the other. "You need to eat more vegetables," he would tell me, blaming me for my motion sickness. I would argue back, "It has to do with the inner ear, there's nothing I can do about it!" I would cite studies that I'd read, trying to appeal to his background as a scientist, but it proved no more effective than later in life, when I cited psychology studies documenting that abuse and trauma had tangible aftereffects, that mental illness was real.

*   *   *

As a child I shared a thin plaster wall with my parents, my bedroom next to theirs. In the years before my father moved back to South Korea, I often heard them arguing in Korean late into the night, my father's deep rumbling mingling with my mother's plaintive tones.

My middle sister told me later that we had, at times, put our own small bodies between them, as a way of calming down their arguments, but this I didn't remember. I do remember the quiet that struck, after much shouting, on the evening when their marriage seemed to split apart.

I was young then, perhaps ten years old. My mother took over my bedroom upstairs. My father sat outside on the wooden stairs, resigned, it seemed. He had fought hard and lost. "Sook, Sook," he called over and over, in a sad lament. My mother ignored his repetition of her abbreviated name. The door stayed closed, and he didn't invade.

Late that night, when she emerged and they spoke without their usual explosiveness, I heard him ask, in English, "What will we tell Imo?"

Imo was my mother's closest family. She was my mother's sister who lived in Canada, the only of our relatives who lived outside of South Korea. I knew next to nothing of her, but that she was the only person my mother spoke to with some regularity. Yet my mother wished to share nothing of my father's pending departure from Colorado for South Korea.

"Why would we tell her anything?" my mother responded. "What business is it of hers?"

Later my mother instructed me in what to say to those who asked. My mother liked to manage things—to come up with scripts for how we should interact with outsiders, strangers. She instructed me in what to say when I answered the phone, how to talk to "Americans." She kept them at arm's length with politeness. It was a lesson I learned early—not to trust others with the truth.

"He moved for work," I parroted to my best friend and her parents. I could feel its lack of truthfulness, even as I repeated this line often. I could feel the way the excuse skimmed over the chaos of my parents' marriage, decaying like atomic particles decomposing and skidding off each other. "His English wasn't good enough to work here."

When I visited their calm house, in the years after he departed the country, my best friend's mother often asked me, "How's your father?"

And I pretended that I had an actual relationship with my father after he left, rather than occasional strained phone conversations, when we spoke for a few minutes. I pretended I knew, as though I, too, came from a stable family.

"How are you?" he would ask.

"I'm okay, how are you?" I would respond.

"I'm fine. Hand me back to your mother," he'd say, and then I could run off again, to whatever I had been doing before the phone rang.

My parents communicated based on needs. He'd request something, "I need you to send me two pairs of Levi's, in this size," that sort of thing, and then he'd disappear again.

My father reappeared sporadically, for short periods during academic breaks, but he didn't interact with us anymore. He would come downstairs from where he holed up in the master bedroom, where he perched himself in front of a small black-and-white TV. I saw him only in the kitchen, getting food, and then he would disappear upstairs into the master bedroom. He didn't speak to me, except to complain about something or other.

My father didn't like Korean food, preferred steak seasoned with just salt, potatoes, McDonald's burgers and fries. But at home he still ate things like tofu, seasoned very simply and grilled, or miso soup. He chided me for cutting the tofu smaller than he liked, once as I cooked, for overcomplicating something that he wanted done just so.

He left cooking to my mother, but he preferred simple things. If you add lots of water to the leftover rice in a rice cooker, and then you boil it, you end up with a mushy porridge—one that you can eat with sliced pickles or jarred jalapeños, as a meal. This meal tastes like sick food, or like survival food. Much of Korean food seems this way—pickled to preserve, vegetable-based, soups and stews designed to stretch hunks of meat into many meals.

In his short reappearances in my life, I heard complaints and criticisms from my father, either directly or passed along through my oldest sister—about how each of us had achieved less success than our parents, despite all our advantages, about how he'd spoiled us. Then he disappeared again, his sharp comments ringing into the void.

As a very young child I was sociable and happy—I was always smiling wide in photos, on metal slides and in swings or at picnic tables, always with some kind of food smeared on my cheeks, usually something sweet like cupcake frosting. In one picture I wear red star-shaped sunglasses, my cheeks wide and pinchable, my hair bowl-cut with bangs, and I look like every other child. Innocent.

This image is hard to reconcile with the disarray that ensued after my father departed the country. My father's presence hadn't brought stability, happiness, or calm; but it had ensured some form of adult capability, even if erratic in form. Once my father departed, what remained was the progression of my mother's undiagnosed illness, as well as that of my middle sister, the two forms often warring with each other.

My father's temper had infected the house—it had been unendurable. I often fled the house, staying in the driveway in the middle hours of the night, because any escape was preferable to being around him. After he left, this departure of temper meant an improvement, in some ways. But the residue remained, in my middle sister, whom he'd beaten with abandon, who'd learned from him how to abuse. Her anger surpassed his.

"You're her sister?" teachers often said to me at school, of my middle sister. They spoke of her admiringly. They saw her brilliance, as ferocious as that of my father's. They saw a polite, quiet person who was somehow much more likeable than me. They didn't see who she became at home, where she sat stewing in rage.

At home she alternated days in which she refused to acknowledge my existence, going without eye contact or saying anything, with days and nights when she flew into furies. She would erupt in fits of screaming, berating my mother for the slightest of perceived wrongs, dinging the wood floors my mother loved so much by tossing heavy items with abandon. In these fits she would destroy as much as she physically could, like a Tasmanian Devil cartoon whirlwinding through the house, throwing anything where it didn't belong, for the sheer purpose of causing distress.

And it worked. I often found my mother crying alone in her closet, a small room lined with ugly brown carpet where she retreated in times of stress. "It's bad for my heart," my mother told me repeatedly, about dealing with my middle sister. "I'm so scared, and my heart. It just pounds, pounds, pounds." She mimicked the gesture on her chest, while saying, again, "I'm afraid."

I felt the need to protect my mother, but I didn't know how to do so. The only thing I knew to do was to serve as witness, to keep a watchful eye at home, to prevent my sister from preying too much on my mother's fearful nature, from getting too out of control. At times I made tape recordings of my sister's outbursts, thinking that this way I had proof of her behavior, before realizing I had no adult figure to whom I could appeal for help, regardless.

And then there were times, too, when my sister frightened me, when I locked myself in the upstairs bathroom for the night, trying to sleep in the hard white porcelain tub, just as my mother locked herself in her master bedroom, as my sister raged. In the days after, my mother would pick up after my sister's mess, restoring the house to some semblance of what it had been before, as though she'd done something wrong and needed to pay penance.

"You're the nice one," my mother told me. Her understanding of the world, and her way of expressing herself in English, were simple. I was the nice one. My middle sister was the smart one. I was the good one. My middle sister was the bad one. Even at the time I realized these designations were harmful ones, to both my middle sister and me, but it was how my mother saw the world.

"You'll see," my mother told me. "It's better to be nice than smart. It'll catch up to her one day. She'll be her own biggest source of unhappiness, her own worst enemy."

My mother had a strange mix of childishness and wisdom that I've never fully understood. She confided in me often, whether I wanted the closeness or not. Her words, though hurtful to my own intelligence, weren't necessarily wrong, in that my sister's behavior seemed destructive to everyone involved, including herself. Where before my family had been undone by my father's temper, in the years after he left, my sister became that figure of fear. My mother lacked the capacity to do anything about the situation.

After my father departed, my mother seemed focused on survival day to day, on staying afloat with her job responsibilities. We rarely had food at home in the years after my father left, the fridge nearly empty but for, at best, milk, orange juice, and fruit. She raised us as though we were tiny adults, already fully capable of figuring out what we needed to know. She did this out of necessity, I think, lacking the bandwidth to do more than try to survive the requirements of her work, so she could provide for us monetarily. Her struggle was more than that of any single parent tasked with raising children—because of her undiagnosed decline, it cost her extra effort to pass at work, to pass as functional in everyday life.

We ate daily from the box of ramen, or "lahmyen," as my mother considered the correct pronunciation, kept in our living room closet. I used to eat it raw, breaking it into chunks in a metal bowl after school. My father, on brief visits home, would get angry over this nutritional choice, even as he'd always left the feeding of us to my mother, before disappearing to Korea again.

My sister often started screaming at my mother over the lack of necessities like food, to which my mother would try cooking something, which she would always ruin. My sister seemed to lack any empathy for my mother, in displaying any understanding of the difficulties she faced.

There was no constancy to my mother's behavior. She was reliably unreliable, even if the ways in which she couldn't be depended on fluctuated over time. I often got stranded in places from which she'd promised to pick me up. She didn't attend any aspect of my life, school-related or social, unless it was related to music—she'd been denied music lessons when she was young, and so, even though I didn't want to play piano or classical instruments, she insisted on music for me. Once I could drive, she occasionally attended my music concerts with me, even as she was reliably absent from any other parentally attended events. I wasn't surprised later in life, when I read that music alleviates symptoms for those with neurocognitive disorders like Alzheimer's—I saw this play out in real time with my mother, as she calmed down whenever she sat nearby as I played piano, often specifically because she asked me to play for her. "Play for me, play for me," she asked me, as she sat expectantly on the floor.

She didn't care for sports, and so sports faded from my life. After my father left, I missed his encouragement of my athletics. My mother couldn't care less about sports, and so I stopped going out for them, became sedentary, as she was. My vision was changing, too, and since no one else noticed anything was wrong, I didn't question why I failed to recognize peers' faces until they were within arm's length, or why I couldn't read the names, written in black marker, on white strips of tape on others' shorts.

"Call out the name of the player you're passing to," our coaches told us, in summertime basketball practice in middle school, but squint though I might, I only saw a blur. I had no one I could talk to about such things—my mother didn't listen when I tried to talk to her about my life, distracted by some facet of surviving her own—and so time went by when I couldn't see, during which I thought life simply was this blurry.

With neurocognitive disorders and mental illness, someone often does need to stand in, in terms of capability, and to pretend otherwise is to diminish caretaking, as well as the real tolls of an individual's impaired abilities. Growing up I became accustomed to standing in for my mother, as much as possible—

to anticipating her needs, and trying to fulfill them. She would make mistakes at all times, meaning my constant alertness was needed, due to their unpredictable nature.

In the King Soopers parking lot she began panicking as the car kept skidding forward, seemingly of its own volition, after she parked. I reached over and slid the gearshift into Park, quickly, quickly. In the moment she failed to understand why the car wasn't cooperating and she froze, helpless—she didn't realize she'd forgotten to put the car in Park before turning off the engine. These sorts of tiny mistakes translated into a feeling that haunted me. I felt a responsibility to my mother, to help look out for her, to maintain constant vigilance over all the small details of everyday life. These sorts of moments led to her increasingly turning to me, in lockstep with my age, from middle school to high school and on. She relied on me to take over for as much as I could on her behalf, so she could be absolved of the responsibility.

Unhealthy as their marriage was, as badly as they both spoke of each other, my mother seemed to fall apart in my father's absence. My father's departure meant that my mother juggled her work as a professor with raising two children, one of whom was capable of scaring her. More damaging, perhaps, was that with his departure came loneliness. The isolation of their shared lives was mirrored in my mother's isolation as a single parent. When her decline began, she had no close relationships with adults who could notice and assist. Her isolation seemed to hasten her descent. She had only her children to turn to, and herself.

In my father's absence, my mother turned to me in ways that retrospectively seemed unhealthy. Even at the time, I didn't appreciate many of my mother's behaviors, but I had no normal against which to compare. I saw my best friend's family, but her household resembled mine not at all.

My mother often slept in my bed, either to use me as a sort of shield when fighting with my father before his departure, or to ward off loneliness. I wanted my own space, but I could never predict when she or my sister might come bursting into my room, unannounced.

She needed help in nearly everything, or so it felt at the time. Some things sound normal, perhaps, such as her paying me a dollar for a household task she needed completed. But they didn't feel normal. It felt as though she needed me to step in and take care of the tasks that her husband would've managed.

She needed me to be strong, when she was fearful. She needed me to take care of her. Gradually I took on more and more of her responsibilities, as she became increasingly unable to manage. In high school I refiled three years of tax returns, after realizing that she'd done them all wrong. Shortly after, I helped her remortgage her house, when I realized errors in the paperwork were set to cost her tens of thousands of dollars. Once I turned sixteen, she turned driving over to me as much as possible.

After she came to me late at night, in a panic over my middle sister's Ivy League tuition bills, I began managing her bank accounts and bills. I began managing her retirement savings.

When I was twenty-one, after she'd been finally diagnosed with early-onset Alzheimer's, I returned home to file her Social Security disability application.

I knew only bits and pieces of my mother's life growing up. So much of my mother's history was lost to me, because she herself could no longer remember the answers to otherwise basic questions, such as what her parents had done for work. I knew she worked on the first computers in Korea, big boxes that filled entire rooms. I knew she worked with the 0-1 punch cards. That she worked in chemistry for some time, too.

That when she was growing up, her father hid, to avoid conscription into the army. And that her mother used her as her safeguard—taking her along when sneaking in to check on her father. I wondered if that's where she learned to do the same with me, to make me into her shield, when things weren't going well with her husband. I knew her by her bitterness toward my father—that characterized their relationship, from both sides.

If I learned unhealthy behaviors from anyone, it was quite possibly from her. I had once enjoyed taking care of her, enjoyed being the "good daughter" whom she praised. But as she continued declining, I felt the fruitlessness of my efforts. I was tired of feeling like her caretaker. I wished she could see my needs and appreciate me for myself, too, rather than as some sort of extension of herself. So much of my identity was built around trying to please her. I failed to imagine a future or life of my own.

*　　*　　*

To say that my middle sister absented herself from any caretaking responsibilities in relation to my mother, over her decades-long illness, is an understatement. I'd never had anything resembling a positive relationship with my middle sister. Our relationship was fraught. When I was in college and after I graduated, my middle sister appealed to me often when dealing with her mental health issues, in all-hours phone calls that pulled me off balance, that ignored my own life as irrelevant, that I never quite knew what to do with. I was ill-equipped for this onslaught of personal emergencies. There's illness, and then there's also personality, and it often felt to me it was the latter that caused conflict.

Until my own health emergency struck in my early thirties, I was treated, perceived, and I thought of myself as one of the "healthy" ones in my family, with all the accompanying caretaking burden, and resentment, of a healthy person in an unhealthy family. Resources are not shared equally when not all are capable of, or interested in, fighting in the same way. I'd grown up with this expectation: my middle sister would be excused from responsibility, while I would be expected to shoulder it.

One afternoon when I was young, in my last year of middle school or first year of high school, I heard my mother on the phone. She sat on the white carpet of the living room, clutching the receiver in one hand and her skull in the other. "Hi, yes, I threw up," I heard her say in a weak voice. "My head hurts, too. I must have fallen off the sofa while I was sleeping, and hit it on the side of the coffee table."

I listened as my mother described her urine flow and whether there was blood in her stool. I heard her shout weakly upstairs, past me, past the banister, to my middle sister. "I need you to drive me to the hospital. After I take a shower."

By the time my mother had finished her shower, my middle sister had conveniently "fallen asleep," her response to my mother's urgent request for help. She'd shut her bedroom door, which my mother and I both knew meant we could not disturb her for fear of inciting her violence. Even as my mother continued pleading for help, she continued pretending she'd fallen so solidly asleep that she couldn't hear a thing. So my mother took me with her to the hospital, instead, in a cab. I spent all day waiting at the hospital, and then into the night. Nurses took my mother away to run tests on her. She didn't say anything as they led her away, and there was nothing to do but to wait and worry. I had brought my geometry textbook with me, tried to study for school, but failed to concentrate. I began hating hospitals at that point in my life, the cold feel of them, big, pale, overly lit shells of buildings. During that time my only comfort was the hot chocolate vending machine, putting in coins, pressing buttons, and watching the machine spurt out two streams of liquid into a paper cup.

When my mother finally emerged, after we transferred to another hospital and then got in a cab to go home, she still didn't tell me anything of what had happened. The cabdriver looked at her and asked if she was going to get sick on the drive home, if she needed a plastic bag, to which she shook her head. I felt as though I were sitting next to a child.

Only when my mother called my oldest sister, her own sister, and my father, did I learn what had happened. "It was a mini-seizure, they think. Or maybe a mini-stroke. They're not sure. But they say I'm fine now."

At home my sister stared straight past us. My middle sister and I lived in different worlds when it came to my mother. For my middle sister, my mother was responsible for her happiness. I, on the other hand, felt I had to look out for my mother's happiness, because clearly no one else was doing it, and my mother was not happy.

Mothers have historically been cultural transmitters. We look to our mothers to teach us how to be.

"Mothers will do anything for their children," someone once told me. My ex-boyfriend's mother, I think. I wanted to argue, but what was the point? If there's anything people assume to be universal, it's a mother's love. That hadn't been my experience. Culpability is one thing—erased, in the delayed recognition of illness. Aftereffect is another.

When you're young, you look to your mother for future possibilities, and in her case, I saw decline. I hungered for the accumulation of memories, because I saw my mother gradually stripped of it. I imagined myself following the same trajectory as her. I wanted to fill myself up to the brim with experience first. I learned later that, as with water from a cup, experiences spill over, displaced by more recent and more vivid moments. I've already forgotten so much.

My parents seemed to believe in the myth of education—that armed with one of sufficient quality, somehow one will arrive at having utility to society. They gave little advice on how to be a good person, or how to move through the world. They were confident that with good enough schooling, we would all figure out the rest. It's hard to overcome the effect of one's socialization at home, though, which is more primal and more fundamental than any lessons learned in the outside world.

7

BUBBLE WRAPS

Money existed in an odd orbit in our household. On the one hand, there was money for things we didn't necessarily want, like private music lessons, and always for school necessities, like AP exams or college application fees. On the other hand, I was always hungry at home, from our lack of food. We didn't buy clothes, forever wearing the same baggy, ill-fitting attire. In retrospect I recognize the sorts of neglect my middle sister and I grew up with as a sign of my mother's illness, more than an element of class. Whether we had money was a different question than whether there was an adult able to spend it as a parent might usually.

There was no constancy or logic to how money was handled in my household. We had it for pet projects of my parents', the random tennis lesson or the music lessons my mother insisted on for us. Education costs were always seen as essential, not optional, regardless of subject matter. But we often didn't have money for basics that others readily spent money on, such as stocking the kitchen with food, buying clothes, eating out, or entertainment.

I brought my girlfriend a present once: leftover packaging material from a box I received in the mail, carried with me on the Greyhound to Chicago.

"So relaxing, don't you think?" she asked the first time I saw her fingers kneading air sacs, elbows out at her sides, *rat-tats* issuing forth, busy as she was massaging the guts of a small padded manila envelope. "Ooh!" she said with glee.

In my childhood household, fixated as we were on conserving, both for the environment's sake, and financially, such things would be saved for reuse, but never enjoyed. In hers bursting bubbles was a special, and rare, form of pleasure.

"Thank you for bringing me bubble wraps," she said. "Thank you."

And she means it—that's the best part of all. She is that innocent. She is that unmaterialistic. She is, in that way, completely different from those I've loved before.

"It's fancy," I tell her, because it's sticky on one side, so she can wrap herself in it, if she wants to, and it will adhere. Later we find the fancier: a clear double-sided pouch we can grab and pinch with both hands, four layers of bubbles rubbing up, twice the *rat-tats* issuing at once.

"There's something childlike about her," my friend says. My friend means this in a disapproving way. But I like that things are still simple, unspoiled. That life's logic is clear. She is, somehow, undamaged.

*　　*　　*

For my mother, safety came in the form of toilet rolls and office supplies. She stuffed the closets and the basements with paper goods, as though such things would ward off danger.

I cleaned the house periodically, filling our driveway with black bags of projector slides and permanent markers and other office supplies she'd hoarded from work, leaving them for Goodwill to pick up. It felt cyclic, where she brought in goods, and I cleaned up after her. She, too, had her own cycle of purging the house—oftentimes throwing away things that I valued, breaking them. Nothing was stable, with her.

Joy came in small forms, too. One of these was coupons. During one stretch of time, she got stacks of coupons for free greeting cards from King Soopers. I accompanied her to the store a bit farther from our house, where the greeting card selection was better. We could only redeem a certain number of coupons each day, so we made repeated trips to peruse and gather. We stockpiled greeting cards, white envelopes and cards cascading from one of the drawers of the wooden chest in our living room. These cards weren't meant to be used, and in fact we never did use them—it was the act of collecting them that my mother enjoyed so much, simply because it was a luxury she could afford.

It was an early lesson that commerce can mean happiness, and that when money concerns loom, there are always ways to while away hours buying things for free. I learned, young, the joys of clipping free coupons from the weekend flier, creating shopping lists based on these free coupons, sometimes filling an entire basket and paying only tax. It was from my mother and her extreme worries about money, worries I couldn't calm by showing her figures or facts. Coupons allowed me to feel as though I, too young to work, could still contribute.

My family was similar to other immigrant families in that daily life wasn't about pleasure or the pursuit of happiness but, more simply, survival. This feeling of survival was separate from practical realities, such as figures on bank statements. It was more of an overriding principle about how to make decisions, day to day, and it changed, over time.

Regardless of bank balances, my family always seemed to live in a different era, one decades behind whatever the norm was in America. When anything broke in the house, at any point over the years, it didn't get fixed, certainly not by a professional. Our house felt like something alive, something in constant need of maintenance. I replaced the interior parts of each of the toilets in our house more times than I can recall, changed the coils in the leaky faucets until they leaked again. When we had electrical issues in the kitchen, my father attempted to fix the wires without turning off the power, resulting in a melted screwdriver and shorted fuses. When the upstairs toilet flooded, a square hole remained in our living room ceiling afterward, where the plaster had been cut out and not replaced. Time and again the plumbing would fail and our basement would flood, and nothing would be done to prevent it from happening again.

Two of the three entryways into our house had broken locks, which could be locked from the interior, but couldn't be unlocked from outside. As a teen I often got locked out of the house, and I'd resort to hoisting my body through the kitchen window, grabbing the chest-height sill and launching myself into the house. There was no one at home, besides me, who was willing to fix things when they broke, or to maintain things, and I was limited in my skill set.

It felt, in our household, as though no one was running it—not the sheer physical space, much less the more spiritual idea of a family unit. In leadership, neither of my parents gave advice socially, on how to be successful in communities or in society. My father gave warnings, instead, on what not to do, or what was corrupt and tainted in South Korea, or, most of all, that I needed to study for my SATs. Education had been his escape route to a better life, and my parents saw education as the one essential, the primary vehicle to a solid life. My father had thought about physiological needs, the bottom of Maslow's pyramid: food, water, warmth, rest. Everything beyond the basic essentials of survival, the bare minimum of financial security—belonging and love, esteem, self-actualization—were completely beyond him.

My mother, on the other hand, was too preoccupied being the breadwinner to take on additional responsibilities. She kept crisp twenty-dollar bills, fresh from the ATM, in a cheap vinyl toiletry bag, a black-and-white patterned thing that looked like a flattened cow, free from the Estée Lauder makeup counter at the mall, in a drawer in the wet bar in our living room. She didn't track how much money was in the bag, only refilled it when it was running low. Her expectation was that when my middle sister or I needed something, we would take money from the drawer and get it for ourselves. It was somehow understood that this was a system of convenience, and that we were being entrusted with responsibility. My best friend growing up envied this system, but I envied hers, in which she got an allowance to spend, rather than access to a resource, without guidance in how to be.

Having access to cash didn't make money feel real. As a child I still undertook tasks around the house for the arbitrary amounts my mother assigned: a dollar to mow the back lawn, a dollar to clean the toilets, a dollar to vacuum the house, a dollar to rake up the leaves. And soon the dollar amounts fell away, as she needed help to keep up with maintaining a household.

My middle sister and I were locked in a strange battle, in which I would do something to help my mother—clean the living room, stack up blankets—and she would undo precisely what I had just done—knock over the blankets I had stacked, purposely create a mess directly after I'd cleaned—simply to antagonize.

My mother assumed certain things about us—that we were a family unit, that our resources were communal, in a way Americans wouldn't understand. My mother's conception of family differed from the more individualistic model of the U.S. She assumed that we would interact and engage in ways similar to her model of family life, that we would each work toward the family's best interests rather than our own individual ones, that fairness would rule.

"I want to buy you your houses one day," she told me with pleasure when I was growing up, because this was how she thought things should be. In Korea most of her family, wives and sons and her parents, remained living in one household.

Emotionally our family didn't play out that way, though. Instead we tug-of-warred over resources, over who spent more where and how. In later years, when my middle sister racked up tens of thousands of dollars in bills routinely, attending college and then dropping out, insisting on enrolling for a second arts degree, then dropping out again, fights were the norm, as we, as a family unit, tried to determine how to pay for these large emergency bills. My mother's model of family didn't take into account the sicknesses that would plague us.

"Does she talk about Malala?" my friend asks.

She and I laugh privately at this innocent question. This is how American media covers Pakistan. This is what we hear. She likes to laugh at how here the script calls for her, as a Muslim woman, as a bisexual Pakistani, to play a certain role—the role of "victim," as she sees it. But it doesn't resemble who she is, not really, not at all.

She is Pakistani, proudly. "Brown is beautiful," she says, with those big eyes, after giving me shit about dating white people nearly exclusively.

She is Muslim. "I didn't think of myself as Muslim until I came here," she says. And I understand precisely what she means. We don't feel *of* something, protective of it, until others who don't have grounds to speak—who *aren't* of it—attack.

"Inshallah," she says, at times. "Mashallah," I respond, or vice versa. "God willing," and "God has willed it," in turn. Or "Haram, haram!" when we do something forbidden.

We joke, but her religion runs deep. When faced with serious troubles, her first response is to pray.

And she's bisexual. She dislikes engaging with queerness as a community, for the way it brings out "types" rather than individuals, but she doesn't mind rainbows. She gives me a bright rainbow monkey T-shirt and delights when women compliment me on it—she knows of *my* discomfort with rainbows, after all. Her playfulness at work, her refusal to take anything seriously.

To those who don't know her, these are the outward ways in which she's meant to identify. And yet there are the more important ways, both large and small. That she still joys in bubble wrap, despite being well on her way to a PhD. Or her sense of wholeness, derived from the family she loves.

"Your amma is so graceful," I tell her once, after studying a photograph of her mother. Her amma is more reserved than her daughter, I can tell, yet she glows with a quiet, calm happiness, her face unlined.

"Buy Laura a present for me," her amma says back, after the comment is passed on.

Her amma could've had a career, trained as she was as a doctor, but she made a different choice. She's cooked nearly every meal for her five children over the past three decades, slapping out chapati daily and boiling black tea leaves in milk for chai, and she cares for two grandchildren similarly now.

Commonplace as these acts of devotion might be in Pakistan, I can't imagine. Love, I think. What it means to grow up in a loving household, with a happy family. What an amulet it provides.

To her amma I am just her daughter's very good friend, the one whom she buses down to Indiana to see every other week, the one who buses to Chicago every alternate week. Who learns bits of Urdu for fun. Who asks for recipes to make for her daughter. Whose daughter is learning to cook, too, and even, despite her disinterest in such things, to drive.

When she spends December in Pakistan, we FaceTime nearly every day. Her large family talks in the background, and they usually know we're chatting.

"Assalam aleikum," I tell her mother, through her daughter.

"Wailakum salaam," I hear back. And more, too—other blessings in Urdu. Her mother is so earnest in her kindness.

"Don't your sisters know?" I ask. "Don't your parents, on some level?"

"No way," she tells me.

I feel guilty at our deception. No matter what we do, back home we will be nothing more than very good friends.

With her Pakistani friends who do know of us as a couple, they see my foreignness, remark on it. "But she's not Pakistani," they say, as though this is a problem insurmountable. "She can't speak the language." At least they are honest about their feelings.

"Oh, you're American, aren't you," her friends say occasionally, turning to me. To undercut their complaints about American culture (or to empathize with my condition, I'm never sure which), they add, "sorry."

In truth I usually feel more comfortable with their perspectives than I do with the average American's. I usually agree with their criticisms.

"I have the best of both worlds," she says of me. "You have an American personality, but Asian values."

At her favorite Pakistani restaurant, the man taking our orders, a non-Pakistani, doesn't understand when she asks in English for three cups of tea.

"Teen chai," I say.

"Ah, teen chai," he agrees.

She and I laugh. She wants me to take over the ordering, so she can hear me stumbling in my American accent. Her culture will never be mine, nor mine hers. It's a relief. It's a relief to date someone who understands the odd composite that is me, who doesn't expect me to explain my cultural inheritance. This, I think, is why she and I get along so easily. We accept each other as experts in our own experience.

I marvel sometimes at her ability to communicate, in human terms, despite her English being less flexible than her Urdu. There's a simplicity that comes with speaking in one's not-home tongue. There's a clarity, too, for a certain kind of thinker.

What appeals to me in being with her is not her "foreignness." It's the way she feels like home. She's similar to what I would've, could've been. When so much is ruled out, it leaves clarity around what is.

She will never marry, she tells me—and certainly never a woman. To be legally recognized in one country means giving official recognition to something that cannot exist in another.

With her country, I run up against the limits of American belief in possibility. It's too intractable there. It's not just about one's own life, she tells me. It's about protecting those one loves—her amma, her baba, her family—from their beliefs in a damaged afterlife, from death threats.

Even though she'll defend Pakistan passionately against any criticism I might voice, against misrepresentations and the ways only certain stories are told, she, too, chafes at the restrictions women face. At the violence, the regressive religious fervor of conservatives. She knows her country won't change anytime soon. She loves it anyway. I came across a quote when researching: "To love a Pakistani is to love Pakistan." This, we agree, is true.

She doesn't have the financial safety net that many here have. Her family is solidly middle-class. A middle-class Pakistani family of five has an income of, let's say, $20,000 a year. She has a different kind of safety net. She understands the power of a close, loving family over an American passport, over wealth. She is firm in her sense of identity. She makes up her own mind about people and things. She is strong.

I want to spend time with her in Pakistan—will, pending the other chaos in my life. It's easier, to tell certain internationals about what's going on in my life. They don't trust the police, understand how dealing with them can wreak havoc.

"You'll probably feel the same way in Pakistan as you did in Egypt or India," she tells me, by which she means the comparable poverty.

She knows of my experiences in Cairo, where a man trailed me through the city's crowded streets, turn after turn, where a policeman I asked for directions assumed I was a prostitute for traveling alone, where I eventually settled for the refuge of a hijab, which rendered me seemingly invisible.

In Egypt I was culturally ignorant, doing all the things I wasn't supposed to do—but the palpability of anger in Cairo's streets was still unmistakable to me, so much so that I wasn't surprised when Arab Spring erupted two weeks later.

"You were there two weeks before the revolution? Ah, you were there during the golden age," an Egyptian acquaintance tells me, with a bitter laugh, to my surprise.

"What did you think of Egypt?" this acquaintance asks me. I can tell she's hardened to the nonsense she hears, from people who know nothing of Egypt aside from their tour-bus adventures to the pyramids.

And I don't know how to say traveling there was the first time I understood the sorts of things my parents felt they'd protected me from by virtue of my American birth. That it was the first time I'd confronted true poverty. That I came to understand the limitations women face, in moving freely and independently, as I became reliant on male traveling partners I met. That as an American who couldn't read Arabic, every street sign meant I was lost. That any description fails, serves only as a projection of my vantage point, and anything more concrete was inaccessible to me. That the way the sun's orange hues bounced off white buildings and smog and flooded the streets of swerving traffic was unlike any other sun I'd seen, even if it was the same.

Poverty wasn't the main thrust shaping my perception of Egypt. It was the anger, the discontent, throbbing at an intensity unmatched elsewhere. In India I confirmed only how much cultural context I lacked. There, after our hired driver knocked over a woman with our car while turning onto a side street in Bangalore's heavy traffic, I glimpsed how differently humans can be valued, based on life circumstance. This is explicitly true here, too, of course—just visible in different ways. He heckled and yelled out the window, rather than offering apologies or assistance. Strangers on the street pulled her aside as our driver kept driving, as we did nothing to intervene.

I have only snapshots of the places through which I've traveled. I had my American privilege, as well as my inability to leave my American judgments aside.

"It'll be different," I tell her. Not just because it's an entirely different culture. "I'll be traveling with you."

On this we agree: we experience places differently through the eyes of those who know and love them. On this we agree, too: that a non-desi American shouldn't bother going to Pakistan alone.

It's funny how after you're reduced, once you're stripped of pride, after you've survived the realization of some of your worst fears, you meet those most capable of love. One of life's compensations, perhaps.

"It's the turmeric," I tease her, after reading a study about curcumin's ability to impair fear responses and treat symptoms of PTSD. I've seen her season nearly everything with the yellow powder. In classic fashion, Americans have since tried to stuff into pill form what others naturally ingest. "That's why you're so chilled out."

We each earn just enough. I could have my freedom taken away from me. She could have her right to live in this country revoked. My country may recognize our right to a relationship, but her country does not. Despite our shared happiness, due to powers beyond our own, our relationship is also insecure.

I know how unpredictable the future is. I know how quickly relationships can warp. And I know, too, despite all of this, how fundamental our relationships are to grounding us on this earth.

She and I know full well the impermanence of built constructions. We choose to build family with each other, anyway. Perhaps just as the sacred and the profane coexist, so, too, does innocence and wide-eyed perception of the world.

8

LINEAGES OF FOOD

My cooking tendencies reflect my own muddled roots. No one style of food predominates, because that wasn't how I was raised.

One day last fall, I stopped by my local Indian/Pakistani grocery store. Since I lived in a rural location, Lafayette, Indiana, I didn't know what to expect. I knew I wanted a wide array of spices—cumin seeds, cardamom, coriander, turmeric, dry ginger, and more.

On my first visit, after taking a few wrong turns, I found the tiny market, which offered little in the way of consumables. The store felt overly lit, bathed in a harsh white light that revealed all the scratches and dinged walls. The commercial chest refrigerator was askew. The metal shelves and wire wall displays were empty save for some knocked over, randomly organized boxes and bags of dry goods and cleaning supplies.

"Come back in a week," the owner told me cheerfully, following me out onto the sidewalk as I turned and walked out the door. "We'll be stocked then."

I nodded, though I didn't think I would return.

"Where are you from?" he asked.

"My parents are Korean," I told him. I knew what he really meant.

"Ah, Korean," he said. "Come back next week."

I came to the grocery store in the first place because I'd made the mistake of telling my new girlfriend I was a good cook. I'd answered her question honestly, without thinking too deeply about it.

"I'll cook for you," I told her. It was only later, when brainstorming what I might be able to cook for her, given her tastes, that I realized I should have been more specific. I'm good at cooking *certain kinds of things*.

In any area of life, surely this is true. We contain indices of knowledge that we fall back on, in the skills we already possess, effortlessly. As a rock climber, for example, I know my strengths and weaknesses in terms of body movements, preferred handgrips, and preferred rock angles. I know my style and its hallmarks, as do most climbers.

At a reading I heard rising-star poet Kaveh Akbar mention how, on a daily basis, we draw upon a bank of three thousand to five thousand words that we use regularly, despite the English language holding so many more possibilities. This is probably why we can so easily identify the language of someone close to us, even if we see only their words, stripped of orality—because we recognize the unique speech patterns they've developed.

Style carries over to the simplest things, including how we communicate. And in cooking, surely the same accumulation of knowledge exists. Just as do other cooks, I know the flavor profiles, techniques, and recipes that I own, as well as those I don't.

"I wanna make you nihari," I told her, in a moment of optimism in my abilities. Never mind that I hadn't yet tasted the dish. Nor had I known, prior to meeting her and hearing her salivate over the dish each week—and then relying on Wikipedia and internet research—that it was the "national dish of Pakistan." I'd never cooked Pakistani food before, but theoretically, it seemed easy enough to make. She laughed at me then, poked fun, but also lit up at the idea.

After looking through recipes online, I told her to ask her mother, whom she said made the best nihari, for the recipe. Her mother's advice? "It's too difficult for her. Tell her to buy a box of Shan's nihari masala and follow the recipe on the back of the box."

"Your mother must be appalled," I said then, "at the idea of me trying to make nihari."

"No," she replied confidently. "An American cooking nihari? She'd be proud."

When I lived in New York City, I cooked frequently, and my spice collection was fully stocked. Whether I sought ingredients for Italian, Thai, or nearly any other cuisine, I knew I had a wealth of options a subway ride away. These were the things I took for granted. I could stop into Sahadi's during lunch break in Brooklyn, or Kalustyan's in Murray Hill, or even trek to Jackson Heights, if I had a craving for seasonal shipments of fruit. A coworker, knowing I was a foodie, once offered to bring me a few alphonso mangos from the stand near her subway stop.

Since relocating to rural Indiana for graduate school, I'd downsized my selection and lived simply. I might need to drive an hour south to Indianapolis, or more than two hours north to Chicago, to find the sort of fully stocked stores I'd once taken for granted. This had been an adjustment for me—the idea that choice meant at least an hour's trek.

A week later I found myself returning to the tiny store two miles from my home, curious to see what its full selection might look like. Surely enough, shelves had been restocked, and though I knew I wouldn't be able to find the whole spices I preferred, a spice blend seemed a possibility.

"Let me know if I can help you find anything," the owner said, smiling at me.

Since he offered, I asked, "Do you have Shan's nihari masala?"

"You know nihari?" His face lit up in genuine surprise and recognition, and he began laughing with pleasure. I looked at him more closely then—at his striped white button-down shirt, at the closely shaved whiskers on his face.

We chatted comfortably after that, about the renovations he had underway, about whether I lived nearby. I left the store thinking about much more than groceries—though the three boxes of spices I bought were remarkably cheap, costing $5 and change. I thought instead about the recognition we each desire—what it means when we feel seen by others, and the ways in which food can serve as a vehicle for feeling known.

When I think how attempts at connection often fail, I think back to when I stayed alone at a hostel in Cairo, two weeks before Arab Spring. My sister and I had decided, as a post-chemo celebration of life, to meet for a wedding in Bangalore and adventure abroad together for the first time. With no preplanning or foresight, I stopped over in Cairo, on the way from travel I'd already embarked on alone. I saw only two other travelers in my time staying there, and I felt lonely and scared. On my way back and forth to the solitary bathroom, I frequently passed a middle-aged white American guest.

We made eye contact, and I said something casual, like "Hi, how are you?" each time I saw him. He, in turn, greeted me respectfully in very proper-sounding Korean and a sort of head bob/bow combination. I had no idea what he was saying, since I don't speak Korean—but I can imagine that for someone who *was* Korean, his politeness would have been very comforting and welcoming.

This nonsensical exchange happened numerous times before something finally clicked, and he realized I was American, just as he was. After that we ducked out of the hostel and grabbed a quick meal of kushari together—an Egyptian dish of rice, macaroni, lentils, tomato sauce, and fried onions—at a casual restaurant where we stood at a table, eating in the open air.

I don't remember the specifics of what we talked about—beyond the time he'd spent in Korea, his work, other idle chitchat. But I do remember how silly our exchanges seemed, until finally I saw the recognition in his eyes—that we, in fact, shared common ground, though on different terrain than what he'd assumed. It was only when he saw me for what I actually was, a fellow American, rather than what he thought I was, that we could relax and bumble along as equally clueless tourists, in search of sustenance.

Sometimes our clumsy attempts to connect, as we make assumptions and projections, only create distance where none was intended. Sometimes it takes admitting what we don't know—our fundamental foreignness as strangers to each other—to see individuals for who we actually are.

When white Americans have asked me, from the time I was little, about what I ate growing up, their statements revealed a certain longing for an easy narrative: of "home" food, in which I dined on traditional Korean food, which my mother then taught me to cook, which I could now cook for these white Americans, in turn. They've offered tidy stories for which they'd like confirmation—that yes, what they know of Koreans or Korean-Americans is essentially accurate.

White Americans frequently volunteer to me, apropos of nothing, that they like kimchi, or that they know bibimbop, or that they love Korean barbeque. At a writer's conference, though my short story had nothing to do with food, my white workshop leader blurted out to me that he liked kimchi—something for which he later apologized.

"That's great," I say blandly, while thinking, "What does that have to do with me? Why am I provoking this particular recollection?"

I feel the same frustration in the insistence of the question I so frequently hear: "No, I mean, where are you *really* from?" Regardless of the question's intentions, its doubt renders me alien. I *am* American. I've often wished that non-Korean-Americans simply asked me different sorts of questions—ones that don't qualify me as somehow foreign, but ones that allow me to define who I am, on my own terms.

Instead, depending on the tone of the questioner as they ask whether I'm Chinese, Japanese, Vietnamese, I find myself mildly correcting by saying *my parents* are Korean; or, if the interrogator is rude enough, insisting I'm from Colorado and ending the conversation.

Yes, I am Korean-American, but my inheritance doesn't fit the neat and tidy parameters of what little is commonly associated with Korean-Americans. My food lineage is messy and complex, as with most individuals, with our own unique amalgamations of past travels, influences, and familial and cultural inheritances. In a place like America, seemingly devoid as it is of a monocultural tradition of food appreciation, this lack of cohesion feels fitting.

I remember an ex's stepmother laughing in surprise, when she learned my Korean short ribs recipe came not from my mother but from the *New York Times*. Despite the assumptions of most who first encounter me, I didn't learn to cook from my mother. At any stage of cooking, I taught myself.

I remember, as a fifth grader, cooking a chocolate cake for my older sister's birthday, from a battered paperback, a red-plaid-covered *Better Homes & Gardens: New Cookbook*, that my mother kept in the top kitchen drawer.

Growing up I remember baking biscuits, adding Crisco to flour, rolling them out on the countertop, and cutting out circles with the floured rim of a glass. I baked these in batches, kept them in plastic bags on the counter until they ran out. I melted slices of orange American cheese over biscuits, for snacks.

Invariably my current or former partners talk of the dishes their mothers or fathers, who cooked for them on a regular basis, made for them. Invariably I visit their homes, where I witness this in action, and where I, in turn, cook for their parents.

Very few of my memories involve parental figures cooking for me. Because for so long my mother needed caretaking, and because I'm estranged from my father—who cooks very little, although he began cooking for my mother in the later stages of her illness—I'm accustomed to thinking of my partners as where I find home.

I think of home as something I build with those whom I love, and as something I find reflected within them. I remember rolling out homemade pizza dough, sautéing onions and mushrooms, dicing jalapeños, squeezing tomato paste, and grating cheese with my ex-boyfriend. I remember slicing purple cabbage, beets, and jicama with my ex-girlfriend, dousing the salad in MCT oil and apple cider vinegar, and sprinkling it with pink salt. These dishes are part of me now, part of my repertoire.

My mother's food consumption was as varied as most of ours would be, if pressed to describe. Her story is not simple. I've seen many cultural influences in the food she craves, and how she craves it. I've seen her relationship to food change over time, in step with her illness.

When I was a teenager, when her decline was well underway, she subsisted mainly on Mr. Goodbar and other Hershey's bars, bought by the boxful. She loved their cheapness—33 cents each, on sale. She loved the sugar. This sweet tooth was both part of her personality, and, as I later discovered, a symptom of mid-stage Alzheimer's.

I vaguely remember, once long ago, that she made home-made doughnuts. I remember her plopping bits of dough into a cast-iron skillet full of cheap vegetable oil, pulling them out with chopsticks, draining them on paper towels. This memory stands out because it happened only once, but it reminds me of how differently she engaged with food before her decline began. These memories are so far afield from the mother who, with all her inconsistency, I mostly knew. I've heard from my older sisters that my mother once enjoyed cooking things like doughnuts.

I don't think of my mother as having cooked Korean food, until smaller memories come back, when I stumble upon a dish she used to make or eat. I remember she did make homemade kimchi on a few occasions—stuffing salted cabbage into large glass jars with plastic lids, squatting on the kitchen floor as she did so, leaving them out to ferment. One batch of cucumber kimchi stored in the basement made me horribly sick—I lost my enthusiasm for eating such things after that.

Then, too, there are a few good memories of foods we shared, when I was very young, almost young enough to forget. These are memories I have to seek out—they are the exception. I remember when I see chestnuts in grocery stores and grab them fondly. I learned that instinct from her. She used to bake them, forgetting to score a few so that they would explode and rattle in the oven. We'd sit together, working patiently, the chestnuts in a metal bowl, another metal bowl waiting. We'd squeeze the chestnuts in dirtied oven mitts, try to separate the inner husk and the harder outer shell from the sweet meat inside. My thumb would get tiny cuts from rubbing against the sharpness of the inner husks, which often stuck unrelentingly to the sweet meat.

I learned, too, how to roast leaves of seaweed from her, though as an adult I rarely use this skill. She'd brush them over the electric coils of our old stovetop, massage the crumbly sheaths in her hands with sesame oil, stack them, fold them into halves and then halves again, quartering them with a serrated knife. As a child I sat next to her, helping her by doing the same.

There are other Korean foods with which I'm familiar, too, ones I was ashamed to eat as a child for the ways they provoked remarks on their perceived oddity from the children around me, including my childhood friends, back before I saw mainstream American culture making gestures toward welcoming diversity. These are foods that are still not commonly associated with Korean culture, because they're the things that are eaten privately, without fanfare. Their textures and specificities are different from what others assume. These foods occupy only a small portion of my cravings, but they're there, nonetheless. They're remarkable only because so few share similar cravings.

My mother was not simply Korean—she was also someone who resisted Korean culture and left it behind as much as she could. We each chafe against aspects of the culture we've inherited, to varying degrees. She wasn't particularly good at cooking Asian dishes—she made a handful of recipes. She was just as passionate about picking up Wendy's chili and Chinese takeout as anything else.

By virtue of being first-generation, perhaps my true inheritance is one of multiplicity. Or perhaps not inheriting a solid food culture simply makes me truly American.

Food inheritance doesn't seem that distant a concept from class, or any of the other abstract concepts we use to arbitrarily classify. We so often press for categorization, but if compelled to honesty, most of us would admit to fluctuations in lifestyle. Who of us hasn't subsisted on ramen and sardines, in hard times? Who hasn't also splurged on relatively fancy meals, in moments of celebration? Who hasn't sought out new flavors or stumbled upon ones by accident, which become ones we then seek out with regularity?

I used to eat at a Yemeni restaurant with a Swedish-Eritrean colleague, with fresh flatbread, foul madammas (fava beans cooked in garlic, tomatoes, and oil, then mashed), hunks of lamb to eat with one's fingers. I hadn't grown up eating such food, but it still felt homey, more honest and real, in a way, than the food that surrounded me in youth—heavily processed, heavily advertised by America's food conglomerates, nostalgic in the way of junk food, but not substantial or healthy—ever has. Good food seems to have more in common than otherwise.

Then, too, I spent a weekend with Russian oligarchs in the Hamptons once. They'd taken a helicopter in from Manhattan. The rock on her finger was massive. My sister was recovering from rounds of chemo, her boyfriend at the time was courting clients, and her boyfriend's friends were visiting. As a house-guest with a tenuous link and little else to contribute, I spent much of my time cooking fancy food, on the fancy professional-grade stove. Lobster, sea scallops, clams from the beach.

As I kept cooking, to my surprise, one of the oligarchs joined in. She corrected me when I nearly threw in the gills along with the exoskeletons, when I made lobster stock for risotto. She took over the kitchen entirely for an evening, made a pot of meat-stuffed cabbage rolls, and another dish, as well, something hearty and meaty, mentioning her experience in restaurants. We never talked of anything weighty, never saw each other again, but food served as the ultimate connector, the ultimate leveler.

These are the sorts of memories that have changed me. The act of cooking is a rare one in which being technically proficient can provide both the basics of human survival—sustenance—and also something equally valuable but intangible. We bring all our past life experience to bear when we cook a meal for someone, when we share. We bring, more importantly, the truth of ourselves forward.

Food can be an opportunity for both novelty in unexpected discoveries and nostalgia. It can be both necessity and indulgence. Wealth doesn't always translate to advantage—in so many other countries, those who are poor can still afford to eat well.

In cooking and in writing, I derive real pleasure and comfort from converting raw material into something finished, something realized. Sustaining oneself might be drudgery—just another example of the many small tasks we must perform. But as with any other task, we can also find joy in executing it well.

Friends used to mock me for being "domestic," in that I like to cook. I'm proud of being able to take care of myself, as well as loved ones, in this way. Food and culture and identity and family and love are tangled together, inseparable.

Generally the skills we teach ourselves are pointless accumulations of knowledge, but for the pleasure we derive from them. Cooking is an act scientific, technical, controlled, and also, in its final surrender to mystery, artistic. Its complexity translates to reward in how there's endless challenge to be found, endless comfort to be taken.

My taste in food has always been for diversity, for variety. I can chart my shifts in diet against the backdrop of my current versus former partners' tastes. My index of recipes is tied to the people and places I've loved. I see this now as a positive—that my food vocabulary is more expansive, for its lack of groundedness in one cultural inheritance.

My ex-boyfriend was influenced by his proudly Sicilian heritage—it was with him that I became accustomed to cooking with pork and wine. My ex-girlfriend was influenced by growing up in Chicago's diversity, by time spent working in Southeast Asia, by her Turkish and Polish heritage. I saw these influences unfold gradually over time, as memories and associations emerged, as stories were told—not by making assumptions or prodding for a particular story. Taking individuals as such often requires asking questions that render us vulnerable and listening without expectation, rather than dictating the terms of conversation.

I grew up hearing only certain kinds of food stories. Writers like Ligaya Mishan, Tejal Rao, Pete Wells, Samin Nosrat are changing those stories—shining spotlights on the places and cuisines that were once ignored in mainstream media, or writing explicitly about their own tangled food inheritances. It's exciting—to see change in the knowledge disseminated.

The more recipes we own, the more we can play when we're in the kitchen. By borrowing bits of vocabulary, we can slowly develop our own points of view, arriving at newness in how we combine flavors.

When my girlfriend and I first started dating, we recognized our lack of a common food vocabulary. My favorite food is Thai, with which she was unfamiliar. I knew close to nothing about Pakistani food, which she told me she'd eat every day, if she could.

The first time I cooked for her, before I attempted nihari, I opted for hearty and healthy: lamb shanks braised in red wine, garlic yogurt sauce, butternut squash, and quinoa. Given her penchant for heavily spiced food, she admitted she found the food "bland."

The reaction surprised me. I'd grown to like simple flavors in sharp relief—the sourness of Greek yogurt, the earthiness of meat cooked with little seasoning, the taste of vegetables roasted for their own sake. Some of my favorite things to cook—mercimek çorbasi, a lentil soup I'd first tasted in Turkey—featured only one or two spices, with lots of acidity.

Then, too, my ex-girlfriend had been allergic to nearly everything, including black pepper and spices. With her I'd gotten accustomed to seasoning with little more than pink salt.

"I'm not like her," she told me. "You can cook whatever you want for me and I'll eat it. Just not pork."

She told me this because she knew of the ways my cooking had changed to accommodate my ex, who'd subscribed to a bulletproof-inspired and gluten-free diet, meaning my grocery bills expanded significantly in buying grass-fed butter and red meat, coconut oil, gluten-free bread, Himalayan salt, MCT oil, and other ingredients I didn't fully understand. But in reality my ex-girlfriend had expressed similar sentiments to my girlfriend's, with an accompanying litany of things she wouldn't eat—things like sesame oil, or ideally no soy sauce, which essentially ruled out most Asian dishes.

"Bacon isn't pork, is it?" I asked. That same ex ate bacon religiously, and so I'd somehow fallen into the habit of eating a sizzling slice every morning, that iconic staple of American breakfast.

In her case, the consumption of pork is explicitly *irreligious*. More than just religion, she scorns it. "Ugh, disgusting," she says, whenever I mention the meat. She considers this scorn a Pakistani norm.

I offered trying to make nihari because I wanted to make something she would actually enjoy, something she loved. And because, too, I wanted to meet her on her own territory, rather than expecting her to meet me on mine.

She shrugged off my offer after I mentioned my difficulty in finding spices, telling me nihari was too much of a hassle to make. But I'd already offered, and the dish still seemed like any other—simple to execute, with a little practice. Shortly after I ate nihari for the first time, I cooked it as a surprise, on one of her weekend visits down from Chicago.

The recipe was simple, on the surface. Making it was a surprisingly laborious adventure, for the sourcing of ingredients more than anything else. I visited the greenmarket farmer from whom I often bought lamb, to get beef shank and marrow bones. He sold me substitute cuts, the closest versions he had.

Then I followed the five instructions on the box as closely as I could. I took out my largest stockpot, measured half a cup of oil, sautéed a kilo of meat along with the nihari masala, added eighteen cups of water and two kilos of marrow bones.

The sheer proportions unsettled me—eighteen cups of water? Surely that couldn't be right. But I had to trust the box, since it was my only guide. I waited six hours, after which I was meant to add one cup of flour, dissolved in two cups of water, and bring everything to a boil for fifteen minutes.

I waited until the last minute to do this, until her train had nearly arrived. My stockpot was already full almost to brimming, so I used far less water to make the slurry. I had a feeling this would cause problems, but I didn't know what difference it might make, exactly. I drove off to pick her up as the pot simmered, told her what I'd made, warned her it was going awry. I cooked for gatherings often; I went against what I already knew in cooking a new dish for a guest, rather than one I was confident in.

"You made me nihari?" she asked, her face softening. "But it takes so long to cook."

I returned to find clots of what looked like fat rising to the surface. I skimmed these clots off, before realizing that the flour was puffing itself into dumpling bits, rather than thickening the stock into gravy, as it was meant to.

"I don't know if it'll taste like nihari," I warned her. "It may not turn out at all."

"It smells like nihari," she said, despite having seen me battle the floating flour clots. The smells were right, but the textures of the dish were all wrong. The gravy never thickened, and so instead the dish became a soup of sorts, with a thinner, watery consistency.

The last step was to fry a whole sliced onion in more oil in a separate pan until golden, and then top the stockpot. This at least I did successfully. Nearly everything else was wrong with my execution of the dish. The tendons in the beef shank become gelatinous, lending the meat a soft quality. The cut I'd gotten was drier, firmer. I served the meat with brown rice, when it's typically eaten with naan.

She said kindly, "The flavors are there.

"It's nihari," she said happily, as she ate. "You made me nihari."

Certain areas of culture are so primal to one's place of birth: language, food. When she speaks in Urdu with family and friends, when she translates for me, I'm reminded of how inaccessible certain fundamental parts of ourselves are to those who don't share places of origin.

Language is harder to learn—I doubt I'll ever learn fluency in languages I'd like to speak, even ones I've studied for decades, like Spanish. Food is a different story. Food is easily shared.

*   *   *

I'm glad for the effort of having made the dish, and I'm also glad to no longer make it. Now I happily join her in eating the nihari that someone else has more capably made. As she tried to warn me, it's a dish well suited to families or restaurants—the proportions too large, the cooking time too long, the ingredients too difficult to buy. We eat often at her favorite Pakistani restaurant, where the surroundings are bare-bones, but the food announces itself. The men working there nearly always slide extra food onto her tray before beckoning her over.

We tear off pieces of freshly made naan from rounds bigger than a plate, pinch bits of beef shank with the bread, drag the same bread through the dark gravy. The dish comes topped with slivers of ginger, with a red oil slick, with a side of raw onions and chopped carrots and jalapeños. These aren't flavors for the timid. Nihari reminds me of Vietnamese beef stew, though with different spices—ones with which I'm not familiar and can't identify, even after having cooked it. I see why she craves this dish—it's fiery, hearty, substantial.

Since then the ways I taste food have changed. As I've embraced the complexity of Pakistani flavors, which once tasted overpowering, other foods often taste bland to me, too.

"Most people I know who like to cook, like to cook for other people," she told me once, and this resonated with my experience of cooking as an act of caretaking, of love. She echoes the sentiment now that she herself has begun cooking.

"I never liked cooking before you," she told me. I've never asked her to, definitely don't expect it—there's nothing like expectation to kill one's desire to cook—but she makes her favorite recipes from childhood, and we share them together.

"It has something to do with home, doesn't it?" I ask, and she agrees. If she doesn't make these dishes, the ones that she can't find in restaurants, she has only the memory of those flavors. Certain dishes can transport us back to a place of childlike innocence.

"It's not just that," she says. "I've never cooked for anyone else before. I like taking care of you."

There's freedom in cooking with someone who has her own lexicon of food. As with most aspects, we're stronger because of the separate narratives we share.

It's become joint discovery, as we introduce each other to ingredients or dishes or techniques. It's flavor I crave, regardless of where it originates. We make odd fusions, adding freshly made pasta to keema (ground beef seasoned with ginger, cilantro, and peas). We substitute rice wine vinegar for tamarind in the quick okra sauté that she loves, talk about bhindi masala's similarity to a South Sudanese okra recipe discussed in the *Times*.

We buy fresh chickpeas and shell them, sauté them in spices, collaborating and taking turns as we cook. Certain things I've learned over time—how to layer flavors, and which flavors I love. I've introduced her to kaffir lime leaf, something I add in thin strips to pancakes, or use to season fish or shrimp or soup.

She cooks with ginger-garlic paste, an ingredient I've never used for its negative associations. For a bit my mother kept large plastic jars of minced garlic on hand; she never learned to cook the rawness out of it, used it only as a shortcut for dishes she didn't want to cook and didn't derive joy from—which translated to largely raw or burnt, inedible food. Now I learn to appreciate those ingredients anew.

I'm learning how little I know of spices and blends. I knew before to begin cooking by tempering spices in warmed oil— this technique is common in Italian and South Asian cuisine. I've learned from her to finish dishes by pouring over tarka— the oil slick in which aromatics like garlic, ginger, and red chili have been sautéed. I've urged her to salt every addition to a pan as she goes, to coax more flavor from what we do agree to use.

Garam masala has always intimidated me—I still don't know what, exactly, is in it. Pot roast was a totally foreign concept when I first started cooking it. Now I update the all-American pot roast I used to make with my midwestern ex-boyfriend, as we cook together out of a slow cooker in a summer basement rental in Chicago. This new version of pot roast, in which garam masala and dried chilis replace oregano and rosemary, cinnamon-y from the masala and sweet from cubed sweet potatoes, tastes like the dish I've wanted all along, without knowing it.

I take a chance on nostalgia one day. For her, mangos are something she rarely buys here, because they fall so short of Pakistani mangos. I understand. So often when I palm mangos in grocery stores here, whether hard or puckered, they smell of nothing. After watching other customers buy cans of mango pulp at Patel Brothers, I purchase the same, despite her skepticism. I open the can, sniff the sweet, fruity ripeness, and know I've won.

"Ooh, that's a mango from back home!" she says. "That's what real mango smells like." We make mango lassi by mixing the pulp with Greek yogurt, drink it greedily, glad for the discovery.

We grab a quick meal in a Korean grocery store, too. You learn more of what others might like to eat by going to grocery stores than restaurants—that's where you'll find the ingredients of home cooking: the fruits and vegetables, the grains, the snacks. As I excitedly share foods with which I do have positive associations—yellow Korean melon, Japanese Botan candy—I realize the dishes we've shared before haven't been Korean or East Asian. It's exciting that we have more to share, more to explore.

She knows I value food—that I couldn't date someone who doesn't appreciate flavor, in all its manifestations. She's the same way. She knows I can cook only a few Korean recipes I've taught myself. She's able to tease me because she knows me as an individual, and because even though our cultural inheritances are separate, they're still somehow linked. We're able to tease each other.

9

POETRY OF THE WORLD

These days I carry with me a purple crystal necklace, hand-made. The man who gave it to me reminds me of a character out of an Agnès Varda film, always foraging and collecting. He buys cashews in fifty-pound increments, fills his rusted white pickup with dumpster-dive hauls. Morels, bike frames, it's all the same.

A world traveler told me once that he kept everything others gave him, for good luck and safe passage. I understand. I carry the black string with me as a talisman, of sorts. It was innocently given, with no expectations attached. Such generosity is rare.

"Why would I ever go back?" my mother used to say, about returning to Korea. Now she's in a nursing home, a train ride away from Seoul. I've asked my oldest sister, a decade older than me, for details, so I can picture it: what sorts of food she eats, what it looks like. I learn only that it doesn't smell of hospital stink, the way nursing homes do here.

I haven't been to Korea in decades, since I was ten. The country is an abstraction to me. My mother's illness has spanned nearly the same length of time. Her illness is not an abstraction to me. Its various manifestations have dominated most of my life.

"You'll regret it," my oldest sister told me, about not returning to my childhood home before my mother departed for Korea. "You'll regret not seeing her."

The truth is, I didn't. I don't.

Our current chain of communication is confusing, stilted. My father, returned in recent years from Korea to Colorado, speaks with my oldest sister in New York, who sends emails to my middle sister, three years older than me, and myself.

He gets updates from Gomo, his sister in Korea, with whom he's had strained relations, but who treks to visit my mother anyway. Gomo's kindness has been variously attributed to religiosity, genuine goodness, or Korean familial values. Any or all could be true. I met Gomo decades ago, just as I did the rest of my extended family. I can't even remember her face.

Nearly as soon as my mother arrived, she contracted aspiration pneumonia, caused from breathing in liquids and particles of food. Pneumonia is common in Alzheimer's patients. In the later stages, the body begins to give out. Certain symptoms are disturbing. They're graphic. The regression mimics a return to infancy, as certain reflexes return: the sucking reflex, and the

Babinksi reflex, involving the feet's reaction to touch. Limb rigidity, when one's arm and hand become fixed in a claw-like position, is the one I most dreaded. These are the visceral manifestations of a slow death.

The hospital treated her for pneumonia and then, to our delayed surprise, placed a feeding tube. After she was returned to her nursing home, my mother pulled out the tube herself.

This act fits with her personality, or the bits unaffected by illness, anyway. She has always been stubborn and strong-willed. It was this determination that saw her rejecting traditional gender roles of her generation and country, in favor of a career—staying up to study by candlelight; programming the first computers in Korea via 0-1 punch cards, on modules the size of a room; relocating to the cornfields of the U.S. to further her education. Later it was this same stubbornness that saw her refusing to leave her job as a tenured professor in Colorado, insisting to my father and oldest sister her mental competency was fine, even as the university that employed her forced her into retirement.

This act fits with the profile of an Alzheimer's patient, too, who responds to medical intervention with confusion. Parsing my mother's personality aside from her illness is similar to sorting seeds from grains. The task is nearly impossible. They overlap.

Now we face decisions anew. The hospital wants to reinsert the feeding tube. If we say no, they will feed her thickened liquids instead, but they won't treat any further instances of pneumonia. They will withhold care.

Relocating my mother back to Korea went against her express wishes. We debated for years. I don't even remember, anymore, what I once believed was right. My arguments ceased mattering. My father, who'd been absent for most of my life, had returned. I was no longer the decision maker. At one point, once the decision was made, I offered to relocate my mother to Korea myself. My father wasn't ready to see her go.

This fight might be easier. My sisters and I are unified in our belief that my mother would not want her life artificially prolonged, that she would not want unnecessary medical intervention. My father will most likely feel the same. This stance is medically endorsed here in the U.S., as a way of reducing patient suffering.

Having such certainty doesn't render the situation less painful—that we've arrived at this juncture, in which the decisions we make dictate how my mother will die. We've reached a new low of lows.

I had a child's belief, once, that if I could make my mother smile and laugh, if I could solve some of her worries, then she would get better. She hadn't been diagnosed then.

She had her yellow sticky notes scattered everywhere, little bits of mind and memory committed to ink. She had the articles she clipped back when papers were delivered in print alone, the ones she highlighted for their information on Alzheimer's and gathered into bundles.

"What's wrong with me? Am I going crazy?" my mother asked me in near-constant refrain, sometimes mourning mistakes she'd made, sometimes simply expressing her angst.

Even as others often explicitly told her she was too young to have the disease, including doctors, she feared she was developing it. She never received confirmation before it was too late.

I fought for her happiness. The more I gave, the more she took. The more she required.

She had the times when, as a child, I would find her crouched in her master bedroom closet, thick brown carpet as backdrop, crying with such intensity that I wondered if she might cause herself serious harm.

Later, in my teenage years, she took to pacing the basement, carrying on lengthy conversations with her brother who wasn't there, rearranging her massive piles of toilet paper for comfort. At times she hoarded paper and other goods, which I periodically gathered for donation before she began rebuilding her supply. At times she purged, throwing out treasured belongings that couldn't be reclaimed.

"We're going to miss trash day!" she said urgently, angrily one day, a few months after I graduated college, when I'd flown home to file her Social Security benefits, as she scooped up garbage in armfuls from our kitchen trash can and carried it out to the front sidewalk, wild look in her eyes. I quickly realized I had better get out of her way. She had times when standing in the way of her obsessions meant facing physical harm. No obstacle would prevent her from getting that garbage to where she felt it belonged.

Always she had times when she was angry and scared, when she stormed in to wake me with her worst fears in the middle of the night, hoping I could solve them. When she pleaded for help. When the entire house was rocked by her tremors.

*   *   *

The first six stages of Alzheimer's encompass psychological torment, the pain of which I witnessed without understanding its cause. Growing up I took care of the practical. I did this mainly because the emotional takes too great a toll. Because witnessing my mother's decline, and being helpless in front of it, devastated.

As a teenager I managed her finances. Refiled her taxes, corrected errors in her mortgage refinance. Paid the bills, set up installment plans for my middle sister's tuition. Drove her when she didn't want to drive. Did household maintenance and tasks. In college I rebalanced her retirement accounts. Put together spreadsheet after spreadsheet, researched meticulously, when she needed help she couldn't request and I couldn't provide.

I took her worries and fears as my own. I lived with her lack of boundaries, with physical discomfort as she encroached on my body and my space. I still question—was it okay she did this thing, or that? Was that natural? Was that normal? Was that wrong? Some things I never speak of. Her shame is my own.

I missed most, but not all, of the seventh stage, in which physical degeneration takes primacy. This final stage is broken down into even more substeps, in which patients lose the ability to speak, use the toilet, and walk; to sit up, hold up their heads, smile, to swallow.

I wasn't willing to change her adult diapers. I wasn't willing to bathe her. I wasn't willing to keep having avoidable emergencies thrust upon me, by those who hadn't listened or granted assistance in caretaking when I needed it, who didn't help enact methods of prevention for those emergencies, who hadn't even believed she was ill until the proof was undeniable. I wasn't willing to keep losing myself in grief. My mother's decline isn't something I can recount, in every agonizing detail. To do so would cost too much. I did what I could, for as long as I could.

So much of my life I thought only in terms of what my mother wanted or needed of me, rather than what I wanted or needed for myself. I served as a vessel for my mother's desires, rather than as a creature of my own.

The best thing I did was finally to say no, to anger and guilt and invocation of duty, and to persist in saying it. The best thing I did was say yes, to taking those first steps toward carving a space for myself.

I've watched my oldest sister grapple with some of the same emotions I faced. I've seen that same letting go, in which she sends photographs of green sunflower seedlings in their small burlap sack on her windowsill and talks of new growth. I can't speak for her journey, can only observe it. Grief is personal and private. We've lashed out along the way. We've found peace, too.

My mother had a similar trajectory. She had her days when she was plagued by doubts. She had her days when she lashed out. And then, too, she arrived, finally, eventually, at some sort of peace. When she sat docilely as I made her a simple dinner of chopped zucchini and yellow squash, white rice, and seasoned ground beef. When she happily ate leaf after leaf of dried seaweed, covered in sesame oil and sprinkled with salt. When horror at life's possibilities had ceded, when recognition itself passed, replaced by the carnal pleasures of the everyday.

My father used to grow angry with my mother for eating entire packets of what's meant to be eaten only as a vehicle for conveying rice, vegetables, and meat. After he became her caretaker, he was simply happy when she ate.

I know now what I didn't know then: that the disease lasts long enough to exhaust us all of caretaking. Of loss. No one can withstand the strain alone. No one should have to. It's not the effort that's so defeating. It's the inevitability of the outcome.

Early-onset Alzheimer's demands surrender. The disease doesn't leap up; it grinds you down slowly. The sadness you're left with is more depression than shock. Whether for sufferer or bystander, the disease seems an endless process of remembering, resisting, and finally letting go.

I write from a primitive campsite I've returned to many times. In the weeks since I last visited someone has fashioned a crude bench, a wet plank balanced on two flat stones. The campsite is, in this way, improved. Litter fills the fire ring—an empty glass bottle, and an empty can of beer. Large insects fling themselves toward my headlamp's illuminations as I type, buzzing against netting. A few find their way in, to rub their slender torsos against the light. A creature screams wild cacklings from the trees, in the dimly lit night. No other parties are here. The stream trickles, as it always does. The air is humid, as usual.

Sometimes the hardest thing is to do nothing. That I didn't return before she left doesn't undercut the ache I feel in being so physically far away, as she approaches death. I can't attach poetic imagery to something that is so brutally unornamented and real. I can only look outward, at the poetry in the rest of the world.

10

WANT

Part One

My life felt like it truly began after I moved to New York City for college. In the city's controlled chaos I could get lost, be anonymous. For the first time I felt I fit in.

I made friends who didn't treat me as a cultural outsider, who weren't white. Many were Asian-American. Those of us not raised on the East Coast bonded over having never had Asian-American friends before. Nearly all were well-off business-school kids, culturally conservative in comparison to writer or climber freaks. Nearly all came from tightly knit communities.

I didn't come from similar wealth, though I became accustomed to rubbing shoulders with it. I was a scholarship kid, one raised on the quiet, open expanses of the West.

My mother had taught me how to take care of her, but she'd taught me next to none of the things most learned from their mothers. I'd paid little attention to what I wanted for myself.

My friends helped me learn the most basic of things—how

to dress, how to be. They took pity on the feral creature I was. I was utterly oblivious. I'd shut off so much of myself emotionally, built myself into something hard and strong. Underneath that armor was a well of sensitivity and vulnerability.

I fumbled when it came to the most basic of questions, because for so long, I'd sought to appease those around me. I'd been in reactive mode since I was a child, and unlearning that has never truly stopped. I made all sorts of mistakes, but they were mine to make.

Once I suggested meeting a friend at a bar in the Village because its location was convenient. I'd been there once before, when I'd met a group of acquaintances for a live music show. On the night I met my friend—my conservative, Christian, Asian-American friend—something seemed different.

A few minutes after showing up I excused myself to the bathroom, which was crowded with women talking about girlfriend drama. In my absence a woman at the bar struck up a conversation with my friend by saying something along the lines of "Is she not treating you right?"

After I returned, as I waited for my friend to wrap up what seemed a random friendly conversation, I chatted with an Australian tourist, a man I later realized was the only one in sight. It was only once she extricated herself and I mentioned the bathroom gossip that we realized something different was swirling around us. We were in a lesbian bar.

"I could never date a woman," she said, looking disgusted. She'd often been mistaken as gay despite being entirely boy-obsessed, something she ascribed to her "athletic" build, square-shouldered and lean. "What about you?"

"I don't know," I replied, without thinking much about the question.

"You don't know?" she said, a frown on her face. I could tell she viewed me differently for my answer, though I meant little by it.

"How would I know?" I replied. As a rule, I dislike ruling anything out. Even if I thought of myself as straight, even if the situation was entirely theoretical, "never" seemed so extreme. How could I know such a thing?

I'd had more pressing concerns—the violence swirling around me, the untreated mental and neurodegenerative illnesses of my middle sister and mother, the void left by my father after his departure for Korea. To be honest, I'd often thought of sexual identity politics as a first-world problem.

My philosophy is and has been simple. I love the person first and foremost. The rest doesn't matter. The idea of love has always seemed a refuge—something precious, untainted. It is that simple, and it isn't.

When I think back to my ex-girlfriend's and my beginnings, I see the damage that can occur when you don't admit to desire. It was only later, after we broke up, that I had emotional space of my own, to think through what our relationship had meant to me. How it had challenged my ideas of love, and of my identity.

It began just as I was preparing to leave the city for grad school in rural Indiana. I'd decided to pursue writing against the advice of nearly everyone I knew. Doing so felt less choice than recognition: my life circumstances had long ago set me apart from my peers, even if we shared the privilege of a good education.

I'd grown up in silence and shame around the strange circumstances of my family life, and I couldn't reconcile it anymore. I wanted to escape the critical voices around me, who were too practical to assign worth to writing or an MFA. I wanted to escape the money-driven nature of the city. I wanted time and psychic space, to think and work.

She was a voice of support. As an artist who'd applied to MFAs multiple times, she understood their allure. We were both restless for something new. She wanted a fresh intellectual challenge. She wanted to stand on her own as a climber, separate from her father's shadow. She saw me first in that light: as a climber.

She'd already left for Los Angeles by the time I set forth. We surprised ourselves with the discovery of each other.

On her thirtieth birthday, she and I spent the evening outside. We'd nestled our campsite between a river and a beautiful cliff band. We hoped to climb the next day. Rain drizzled on us, but still, we hung out by the fire, ate heat-lamp roast chicken and avocado slices with our fingers. I chilled a bottle of sparkling wine in the river, and we toasted out of matching *Sesame Street* cups.

We'd jammed a queen-size air mattress into her orange tent, and we crawled in to wait out the weather. That night, sounds of rain drummed down on us endlessly, but when we woke, snow greeted us. White glitter had frosted the tent, the trees, the crag, the vista. It meant we couldn't climb, but we didn't care. We went to natural hot springs and sat steaming, instead, as the cold air bit our faces. It was April in Wyoming. We were just friends then.

On my thirtieth birthday, she and I searched fruitlessly, at the wrong dirt turnout, for natural hot springs in small-town Utah. That night I saw my first shooting star. *A birthday gift from the universe*, she said. A few days later, we stumbled upon a lamb-eating festival, in a tiny town that once communally owned a hundred thousand head of sheep. The locals recognized us after the first day. They chatted with us kindly, laughed when we mispronounced the names of nearby Mormon-settled towns, helped us understand important details of the lamb-sandwich ordering system, justified the number of lambs they'd decided to roast in the pit that year.

She and I laughed privately, in turn, at the men who wore pink-and-white-striped aprons and drank Mountain Dew rather than beer as they barbequed. We marveled at the lamb auctioneer and gorged on sourdough fry-bread. We stroked lush sheepskins. We climbed hard each day of the festival, listening to Jeff Buckley as we drove into the crags, and then stuffed ourselves full of lamb to recover. It was July in Mormon country. We weren't lovers yet.

We spent the summer together, endlessly extending our trip. We meant to write a collaborative proposal for an artist residency, for the following summer—we even sat on tractor tires together under the moon, in a random playground in a random town, taking notes on each other's ideas.

In moments when we weren't working, climbing, or making things, we talked about life and love, writing and art and music, usually in front of a campfire, stars as the backdrop. This was remarkable, to me and to her—that we could share all these things. That hadn't been either of our experience in the past— the *totality of the experience*, as she put it.

The man I'd spent the past decade with and I had decided to part. We'd tested it once before. This time, we both knew the break was final. She had known he and I were on the rocks, and she gave me love advice. *You should be with an artist*, she told me. *It's how your mind works.*

Given she was one, I took her advice seriously.

She'd been with the same man for eight years. At times she seemed frustrated with his lack of interest in ideas, his fear of adventure, but those moments faded quickly. *I'm basically married*, she'd told me cheerfully on a few occasions. Just as she told me frequently, somewhat randomly and seemingly unprompted, *I'm straight*.

On a rest day, we sat on rocks in a dry streambed, as she made field recordings and sketches, and I jotted down notes for an essay. On a climb day, after we warmed up, she belayed me on a hundred-foot climb, 5.12c, severely overhanging. The rock was conglomerate; misshapen bowling balls and other slippery protrusions stuck out. The route required nearly twenty quickdraws that jangled against each other as I climbed. When she lowered me, I landed twenty or twenty-five feet away from her, due to the angle. The climb was *above her pay grade*, as she put it, and so I belayed her on a different line. She made a field recording while I climbed, which she later incorporated into a track.

The day seemed representative of our passions. I'd been climbing for twelve years—it had been a fount of happiness, my first love. I'd loved sports and wilderness since I was a child, had weight-lifted as a teen. Athletics had been my escape. I'd lived solo out of a tent, on the road, for months at a time.

She, on the other hand, had grown up in Chicago's rave scene. Her father had foisted climbing upon her ever since she was a child, but until recently, she hadn't owned it as central to her own identity. She'd DJed in Chicago, Montreal, New York, LA, made electronic music now. As she said wryly, many of her friends were *international techno gods*. Unlike her, I knew nothing about the DJ scene, but I'd been classically trained in music, rather against my will. Just as with climbing, we spoke variations of the same language.

The first time I felt protective of her was in Wyoming. We were relaxing between climbs—no other people in sight, just orange-streaked limestone. We were discussing whether to pay $2 for entry to the local pool, so we could use the showers. That was when she told me about being laughed at in public swimming pools—how when she was younger, groups of children would point at her and yell things like, "Look, Mom, there's a boy in the girls' locker room!"

She said this with a smile, without bitterness, while saying, lightheartedly, that she still had a phobia of public swimming pools. Had she not told me, I wouldn't have guessed—she moved through the world without evident self-consciousness.

I understood it as the accidental cruelty of children. But still. I could imagine the sting. I wished, for the sake of this girl in front of me—whose spirit is beautiful, whose exterior is beautiful—that she could've been accepted as she was.

The first time she felt protective of me was when we met up in Utah. I'd just visited my mother in Colorado. I tried to act normal—to suppress my hurt, as I usually did—but I couldn't. We'd rented and shared a small room for the month, with an attached sitting area, which we used as our home base. The first time we touched, she moved to sit next to me on the floor, our backs pressed against the baseboard. She reached out to hold my hand awkwardly, as I cried.

It was the end of our first trip. We'd been to natural hot springs together before, of course, where the atmosphere was meditative, nearly religious. But the vibe was different in the indoor hot tub of an airport hotel, plastic cups of homemade Manhattans in hand. It felt both trashy—in the way of airport hotels—and also celebratory. Politeness inevitably wears thin on climbing trips, when nearly every minute of every day is spent in each other's company. Yet on this trip, chemistry had been effortless.

I took off my shirt and got in first, sat down. As she descended the stairs, I remember being conscious of her body, as well as of her being conscious of mine. As she put it, *there was tension.* We both felt it, but we didn't know how to locate it. We both, after all, identified as straight.

I had the excuse of looking at her tattoos, which drew my eye. Words curved over each hip, and a husky covered nearly her entire upper leg. I was surprised, too, by how delicate she was. Her arms are whip-strong, her demeanor confident. I hadn't seen her so exposed before. Or, perhaps, I hadn't truly looked. She told me, too, that she hadn't fully realized until then *how good you are at hiding your body.*

We'd both been conscious of each other's energies, when we first met, on a shared shift at work. *I knew I didn't want to fuck with you,* she told me. *You're intimidating.* She associated me with *power,* too. Yet she also told me that she could tell I was hiding, that I'd been hurt, that my spirit was gentle.

I felt the same way about her. That though her exterior suited her—the leather jacket, the messy hair, the piercings, the tattoos—it also served to conceal. I assumed she projected a tough exterior as a shield, meant to protect a sensitive spirit. I could read her intelligence, her curiosity, too.

We both saw through each other's acts partially because we both did the same thing, in different ways, for different reasons—used the exterior as a way of protecting ourselves. Yet even still, we were both surprised by what lay beneath.

She and I traveled through so many geographies that it blurred—over a third of the U.S. Somewhere along the way, we fell in love. In looking back, it felt as though we'd been attracted to each other since the moment we met. We just hadn't admitted it to ourselves. It grew from there.

We parted ways in mid-August. I dropped her off in Chicago's Union Station; she burst into tears on the train. She flew back to LA, where her bandmate had flown out for an intensive week of recording music with her and her boyfriend.

She and her boyfriend shared a three-bedroom house in LA, backyard overflowing with avocado, mango, grapefruit, and Meyer lemon trees. They'd poured love and sweat equity into their home, in exchange for cheap rent.

I had meant to arrive at grad school orientation focused, eager, and ready to write fiction. Instead I spent the entire time filling my notebook with confusion about and longing for her. She wrote lyrics about us, recorded them Laurie Anderson–style.

You're in love with her, aren't you, her boyfriend said, able to see it before she could admit it to him. *I'd be less hurt if you left me for a woman. Look, I get it. She's a climber, she's an intellectual. She's all the things I'm not.*

She and I existed outside of space—we were always travelers together, rather than rooted solidly. She had someone anchoring her. I felt guilt, then and now.

As long as it's not hurting anyone, what's the problem? she said often, about her openness to various ways of being.

The problem was, our relationship was hurting someone— her boyfriend, each of us.

He is, undeniably, a good man. Their house was filled with love. He didn't deserve to have his life thrown into chaos.

The situation was a departure, for both of us. Had either of us been male, we wouldn't have let down our guard, wouldn't have formed the emotional intimacy that we did. Neither of us had ever cheated on anyone.

She and I would talk for hours. He knew when we were talking. That period of indecision was torturous. We discussed every option; she wanted to find a compromise, in which we could all be happy. She wanted to love both of us and hurt neither of us—an impossibility.

I could understand how she could love him and me simultaneously, and I also couldn't. I couldn't because she was enough for me, and more. The same seemed true for him. I wanted to be the same for her. I wanted to be enough.

Before we began, she made paintings inspired by us, based on electricity, in which graphite lines snapped and sparkled, shone with energy. The lines are dense and tangled, as our relationship was—many different forces colliding. *They're yours*, she told me. *I made them for you, about you.* I knew what she meant, because I was also making work for, and about, her.

In the original painting, one line sticks out, like a tuft of hair from her head. It's in keeping with her belief in imperfection— that it's what doesn't fit, what isn't controlled, that makes a work interesting.

In real life, the imperfection was clear. I believed in solid foundations, in doing things the right way. It bothered me that we were doing things so wrongly—and yet I couldn't walk away. With her, falling in love wasn't a choice. It felt scarily the opposite—a force to which I was powerless. Undeniably there, in a way I hadn't experienced before, in a way I couldn't—and can't—explain.

Oddly, it had something to do with trust. We could read each other on a level that wouldn't allow for lies. It had something to do with want, too—with seeing her desire, matched by my own.

You never know what you might get, if you share what you want, she told me over the phone.

The experience was new to me: of being asked what I wanted, of it mattering.

When we finally saw each other, there was so much nervousness. She broke up her life with him on faith. When we finally touched each other, there was such confirmation. Our chemistry was undeniable.

The first time we kissed, I remember pulling back in surprise, turning away and mouthing quietly, *Oh, fuck.*

And her saying, nearly at the same time, *Yeah, we're fucked.*

Dating her had something to do with allowing myself desire, desire inexplicable, for the sheer sake of it. It flooded us. Everything was new, exciting.

It's like we're teenagers again, she said.

We brought to bear all the fractures we'd experienced, all our complexities. This was both our strength and our weakness:

our differences from each other, our complexities, and the difficulties we'd faced. We recognized in each other something we hadn't shared with others—the degree to which neither of us had felt accepted as we were.

I don't trust women as much as men, she said. Somewhat offended, defensive on behalf of womankind, I asked her what she meant. *Women are way more aggressive than men.*

This sentiment horrified me. I was fed up with the surely universal female experience of being objectified and propositioned inappropriately by men. So many, including friends, seemed to see only what they wanted to see—the physical body, the exterior. *I'm so sick of men*, I told her. I distrusted their intentions.

She, on the other hand, felt objectified by women. *You can't possibly be straight*, she'd been told. She felt women had little interest in her as an individual, yet still wanted to sleep with her based on physical appearance alone. She'd been propositioned by more women than she could recall.

She'd gotten used to vocally declaring her *straightness*, due, in large part, to assumptions others made about her sexuality. *I've had a conflicted relationship with my sexuality*, she told me. I could understand why. I could see the damage those assumptions had done. She felt she'd made a conscious decision. That she'd *chosen* to be straight. She compared it to choosing to go through one door and closing other doors.

This difference in lived experience fascinated me. Partially because our comparisons made clear that the question of who possesses the Gaze is irrelevant. It's the Gaze itself, when wielded violently, that can be destructive.

She told me later that it wasn't just children in public swimming pools who commented on her appearance. It was teachers at her small school, who yelled at her for being in the girls' bathroom, who told her she didn't belong. Those sorts of incidents occurred frequently.

By violent, I mean, perhaps, that when we vocally define others' personhoods to them, when we essentialize, we are capable of causing great harm. Telling someone that s/he *can't possibly be straight*, or gay, bisexual, or unlabeled, female or male or nonbinary, or any variation, feels no different than my mother telling me, *You're too stupid*. Or my father making fun of what he saw as my *chubby thighs*, or telling me, *You're a girl: you're too weak*. These comments are corrosive.

Throughout our trips, she and I were always just two strangers passing through, too transient to invite real commentary. We often had the luxury of forgetting that the outside world existed. The only gaze that mattered was each other's.

In rural gas stations and the like, of course, she attracted plenty of stares. I did, too. Individually, we are both used to it—to being seen as different. Growing up Asian-American in Colorado, I received more comments than I care to recall, issued from close friends and strangers alike. Just as her presence in public spaces had attracted commentary, so, too, had my own.

Peers asked why my face was so flat, or commented on what they saw as my *squinty, slanted* eyes. Substitute teachers asked me slowly if I spoke English. Strangers approached to ask if I missed China. *Ching chong ching chong* yells greeted me from moving cars.

As a frequent traveler, I am well aware that how I am seen changes, based on geography. When I was an adult crossing into Turkey, the border guard refused my U.S. passport repeatedly. He wanted my *other* passport.

When I am the only person of color in a given space, I am always conscious of that fact. I am aware, too, that the presence of my visage might draw unwelcome comments, wherever I go.

I remarked to her once, when we were driving through East LA, that I was pleasantly surprised by how little commentary we'd gotten on our relationship, at least from strangers. In bars, on trains, walking in city streets, we'd gotten stares when publicly affectionate—some friendly, some unfriendly—but little more. She turned to me and said seriously, *Yeah, but you know it's coming.*

I knew what she meant. I hoped she was wrong. Then and now, a boundary-less view of sexuality and desire has brought me joy. It's made me more human. My sexual fluidity isn't as readily, visibly apparent as my ethnicity, and therefore it's been less likely to cause unwelcome commentary. It has felt like a source of strength I've gotten to choose to share.

Racist comments wounded me when I was young and vulnerable, partially because they mirrored my reality of ethnic isolation. Nearly everyone around me was white, and so I therefore had to deal with suspicion simply for looking different, in ways I still encounter regularly and deal with today.

Like trauma and illness, dealing with explicit hate is different as a child versus as an adult. As someone who once identified as straight, I find myself less likely to care about openly homophobic comments. I have the emotional distance to judge those comments as what they are—reflective of the speaker; hateful, pointless. Still, I hoped the walls built in response to racist comments, in response to abusive comments from family, didn't have to be built up to guard my sexuality, too.

As someone who grew up buffeted by abusive comments, it took me years to realize that I get to define myself—that others' limitations of my mind, body, or abilities aren't real.

Unlike my ethnicity, unlike my family, being in a relationship with her represented freedom: it was something I got to choose. I hoped to preserve its innocence.

When I arrived in rural Indiana, prior to Trump's election, I saw a polarization that didn't exist in New York City, where the default assumption seemed to be that people were whatever they were: a mix of many different traits and identities. I didn't hear academic buzzwords like *intersectionality* used in conversation. If anything, diversity and difference were the norm. I loved that freedom to simply be, and to allow others the same courtesy. I'd come to take it for granted.

In Indiana I felt pressure to label myself, to identify with either the straight or queer community, and to declare myself right away, as others did. This occurred academically and socially.

In my initial encounters with peers, I was surprised by how many identified vocally as queer—surprised not because they were queer, but because they felt compelled to declare aspects of their identity so immediately. It felt akin to her telling me, *I'm straight.*

After we became friends, I asked one of my peers about her strident queerness. *This is my identity in Lafayette*, she responded knowingly. *It isn't my identity in Portland, or Seattle.*

As someone who has never identified with or trusted group identities, who only figured out as a thirty-year-old how to say the order of the letters in LGBTQ correctly out loud, it felt dishonest to claim knowledge of a collective with which I didn't identify. Yet it felt dishonest, too, to claim no experience of knowing what it is to love a woman.

My aversion to group identities is a lifelong trait. I've never encountered a group whose rules I felt I could wholly abide or endorse. I'm wary of subjugating individual consciousness to the whims of a group. I wonder if any group label can truly allow individuals to embrace all their complexities and quirks, without compromise.

I've often been surprised, and touched, by the protectiveness and generosity of those who identify vocally as queer. I've seen how queerness can make space for others, to exist as they are. Yet I've seen the downsides, too: the ways that protectiveness can lead to overdetermination of others' identities, to dismissiveness, to gatekeeping, to control.

In relation to my sexuality, I'm hesitant to accept any dominant narrative as my own. Internally, my beliefs and values didn't shift significantly. What I dread, instead, is confronting shifts in how my identity is perceived externally, and retold to me. Those most likely to tell me who I am have been those who identify as queer, not straight.

For myself, I believe labels applied by others do not accurately capture my experience. I believe that for many women, including myself, sexuality is fluid, not binary and divided.

I feel the same way about my sexuality as I do about being Asian-American, or being female. That I don't move through my day thinking of myself as Asian or as female, until someone else treats me noticeably as such.

I'm impatient with the need to divide identity into categories, for convenience, for the sake of the outside gaze. I think of myself as infinitely changeable, not as a fixed entity. I believe in possibility. I didn't think of my relationship as being primarily same-sex in nature, until I saw how we were perceived by others, when together in public. It is only under the Gaze—of strangers, or at times, each other—that she or I remembered.

Behind closed doors, too, it was undeniable that we were both women. Gender was a part of our relationship that added its own complexities, joys, and confusions. Yet that—gender—wasn't the primary foundation of our relationship, either, any more than sex was.

Unlike her, I hadn't been tortured by my sexuality. My life had been overshadowed, instead, by the illnesses and violence of my family.

I wish I could take away all your pain, she told me once.

I told her in turn, *I wish you didn't have to bear witness to it.*

But I told her, too, because I know it is true, that *it will always be a part of me.* That pain doesn't go away. Yet her willingness to see all of me, without turning away, and her desire to do so with care, helped me heal.

She was the first person with whom I could be both unapologetically strong, and unapologetically broken and hurt, too. She could see that my strength and weakness originated from the same place.

When she asked me later what I wanted from our relationship, I told her, *I'm so used to love that takes. I want love that doesn't take.*

When she told her father that she'd *never known love like this before*, his response was gentle.

That kind of love comes along once in your lifetime, if you're lucky, he told her. *Cherish it.*

I, too, hadn't known that kind of love could exist—without compartments, without barriers, just the fusion of all the things. She was the person with whom I could go to raves or symphonies, wilderness or cities, museums or readings.

I wouldn't want to subtract any one element, or to overprivilege any singular aspect. To do so would be reductive. Something—the intangibles of chemistry, perhaps—would be lost.

I don't identify with either male or female, she told me. She recognized androgyny as a state of being in herself. *Even though, of course, I'm female.* In other moments she said jokingly, *I was basically a little boy when I was a kid.*

Unlike her, I hadn't been mistaken for a boy. But I, too, believe gender is a social construct. I, too, believe in the androgynous mind—particularly for art. *Being an artist is my gender*, Mary Ruefle said in a Q&A, and I agree. With her I believed more strongly than ever that love *itself* is ungendered. Love is intersectional.

The surety in our relationship came not from individual aspects of our identities, not from the wounds we carried, but from confidence: that we could love each other as we needed. That we could share in each other's joy. That we could heal each other.

We never did finish writing the artist residency proposal. Our best form of collaboration had been, quite simply, in loving and supporting each other.

For both of us, our relationship allowed us to reclaim parts of ourselves. For her it meant reclaiming her sexuality, climbing, and the centrality of intellect to her soul. She worked anew toward her dreams of an art MFA, edited her portfolio and artist statement, attended her top pick.

For me it meant moving into myself unapologetically and giving myself permission: to write, to value happiness, to choose faith over doubt or criticism, to choose, however temporarily, self-worth over the power of negative commentary and judgment.

For both of us, our relationship meant shedding layers of defense. In receiving each other's gaze, in being seen fully, in confronting each other honestly, there was nowhere to hide. *Stop hiding*, we told each other, with regard to different aspects of our lives.

This nakedness allowed us to access new understandings of not only ourselves—and our work, and our creative visions—but also of how boundless, rewarding, and generous love can be.

Part Two

If our beginnings were tangled and complex, our ending was infinitely more so. The ways in which our relationship imploded would require its own essay.

I wanted to believe that a first queer relationship didn't have to be tragic. I wanted to write a happy essay about love. Life interfered.

When queer people heard of our breakup, I received more than one knowing nod. "First queer relationship," I heard, alongside comments about how unsurprising it was that it ended in catastrophic fashion. A shorthand, subjective version of our ending might include her stepmother and father's dislike and disapproval; resultant friction in our relationship, from which we couldn't recover; our breakup; and, in the days after, her father's death in a tragic accident.

Even so, I can't ascribe our relationship to a category like mistake or regret. There was an inevitability to it. We met as our suppressed desires were surfacing and intersecting, as new worlds were opening—for me, writing and art and emotion; for her, climbing and a return to intellectual pursuits.

I still have the sheepskin rug she gave me, a handful of her paintings on my walls. Life moves on, but these vestiges remain. They remind me we shared something beautiful, once.

11

GOLDEN DAYS

There are the days, after a walk on the elevated abandoned-then-converted train track a few blocks from our apartment, snowflakes blowing and slapping me lightly in the face as I walk, when I lie next to my girlfriend in bed, her lips moving slowly as she reads words aloud from her book, edited by my mentor, me reading essays as research for the book I need to complete. She shares opinions on each story as she reads. I share stories about the workshop drama mentioned in the book's introduction. We snack on popcorn, salted and garlic-powdered and dusted with nutritional yeast. I wonder, if, despite everything, these are my golden days, our golden days.

As soon as I uncovered the diagnosis, on a piece of paper, while I was sorting through my latest mess of medical bills, I texted her the news. She was in Abu Dhabi, en route to her family and home. We received the diagnosis, both of us, absorbed the shocks separately.

The month we spend apart clarifies this fact: we want each other for the right reasons. Our happiness is genuine, and it's intensified in light of health emergencies, not diminished. We're happy as two otters in each other's company, slipping and sliding and tucking their paws under their chins. I can't point to grand gestures to signify. Love comes in simple forms.

My best work has always included her. Nothing comes across so clearly in nonfiction writing as intention. To us, at least, the pureness of our intentions for each other is clear. But then I wonder, too, how pure love can be, once need enters the equation. That's why these days feel the golden ones—because the truth is known, life is hard, and yet. And yet we're still happy as we ever were, stronger than we've ever been.

This is remarkable given everything that's happened in months prior. I signed with a literary agent; sold my first book; due to the possibility of such a sale, suffered a fracturing blow to my tenuous remaining relationship with one of my sisters. I received word of my mother's worsening condition. I landed in a state-run mental hospital. I lost my mother to her decades-long degeneration from early-onset Alzheimer's. My girlfriend and I moved in the middle of Chicago winter from one apartment to another, after conflict with our previous landlord over a heating system that was never fully constructed, an electrical system that was never brought to code, rat feces making us both ill, cockroaches, and every other plague. This litany might seem unrelated, but for the diagnosis: schizophrenia. A disease in which episodes are triggered by stress, by family hostility and turbulence, by triggering of past childhood trauma, by the death of a parent, by economic adversity such as we faced with our landlord. A disease, too, whose risk factors paralleled many of the themes I'd been writing about: childhood trauma, abuse, ethnic isolation.

In the hospital and in the lead-up to checking myself in, I was afraid of everything, including my girlfriend. She was the one who convinced me to commit myself voluntarily, who tricked me into going into the hospital by claiming that she felt sick. My second episode was the first time my mental illness intruded on the life we built together, in tangible ways, in real-time. She and I experienced, in tandem, two different versions of the same reality.

In the first emergency room we went to, she explained to doctors what she knew of my history, from before we met: a first psychotic episode, a suicide attempt. To her frustration, they didn't listen to her, the person who knew me best, when she said something was wrong. Instead they chalked up my combative-ness to personality, discharged me with nothing more than a headache and insomnia written in the treatment notes.

I landed at another ER after I worsened, after my girlfriend called an ambulance. She explained my history again, and this time the doctors listened. I took an Ativan, which helped me sleep, but did nothing for my suspiciousness, my distrust. She reached out to my oldest sister to learn the medications I'd been on in my previous episode, and again, doctors listened to the in-formation she passed on, and this time I got the help I needed.

Other, lesser, more self-protective people would've walked away. Unfamiliar with the coldness of American institutions, the rules that barred her from sharing with me what she'd made with love, she made kaali dal later and brought it to the hospital, instead.

During this time I was lost in my own nightmares, which I didn't share with anyone. This, I think, is why people stigmatize and fear diseases like schizophrenia so much—because they sympathize with the people who have to deal with the outbursts and symptoms, rather than the person with the disease.

It was my girlfriend's presence during this episode that clarified what I hadn't understood the first time around. I could reconstruct the narrative, both my own crossing from reality to unreality, as well as from her perspective.

"They don't know your personality, so they don't know you're different," she told me, about the doctors she encountered, those who ignored her words. As events unfolded and after, she was fed up with the American medical system and its unpreparedness for mental health emergencies. "It's so obvious, when you're fine and when you're not."

My girlfriend experienced the same frustrations I'd experienced with my mother's illness, which my oldest sister and father had refused to acknowledge, and which doctors had, as well. Throughout my teens and early twenties I'd been the unwilling caretaker for my mother, in the decade before she was diagnosed with early-onset Alzheimer's. I resented it. I resented dealing with my middle sister, too, both her temperament and her struggles with an undiagnosed mental condition, because of the toll taken on me. I was young. Given my youth, as the youngest in the family, and my general quietness, I had been easy to ignore.

My mother went to the doctor unaccompanied. My oldest sister and father didn't live with my mother's behavior and changing personality, or her, day to day, and they chose not to pay attention to my warnings. They left me to deal with her fears and her caretaking, on my own.

As I recovered from my episode, I could see shadows of my mother's behavior in my own in my weeks alone at home. I wondered if I would be able to take care of myself, to cook again, to live independently. I remembered her checking ten or twenty times in a day if she'd turned off the stove. I remembered her burning dishes, rendering them inedible by leaving out nearly all the ingredients. I remembered my middle sister shrieking for hours, when the food was burned.

When I received my own diagnosis, I cried as much for my girlfriend as myself. I knew all too well what it is, to be on the other side—to be the "healthy" person, the voice of reason, bearing the weight of responsibilities invisible outside the home.

"It makes more sense now," my girlfriend told me after seeing me in an episode. Before my diagnosis, my prior suicide attempt hadn't made sense, to either of us. She'd said before, "You love life more than anyone I know."

Even in the moments where I had been trying to end my life, because it seemed the best, the only option, I was also aware I didn't want to. I simply wanted not to feel unsafe. I didn't want to feel as though others were out to hurt me, and I felt I had no other options remaining.

My actions hadn't fit with my background as an average, well-educated individual; nor had the legal problems I'd incurred as a result. Now, with the clarifying lens of diagnosis, my past did make sense, as a typical trajectory for someone with schizophrenia. As with my mother, the degree to which I am cognitively high functioning masked my condition.

*   *   *

I've always written because I wanted so desperately to be understood. Because that's something family hadn't granted me, and because it's so rare to encounter people who understand me innately, without verbalization. My whole life is wrapped up in writing, in this work.

Having my brain taken away from me, when it's what my sense of self and livelihood depends on, felt like a cruel joke, much as it seemed a cruel joke with my professor mother. Perhaps the brain is like a muscle, in that it breaks down when overused.

After my first psychotic episode, my oldest sister and I talked of completing an application for disability. "It's better to start now," she advised me, according to what she'd found. Then we set it aside and didn't talk of it again.

After my second episode I began looking through all the contradictory rules. I'd done this application before, for my mother, just as I'd accompanied my father as he applied for the Social Security benefits for which my mother's record made him eligible. I had next to nothing in my bank account, living on money from my IRA, and my girlfriend was totally broke, too. I have tens of thousands of dollars in bills, racked up from my two episodes—the ERs, ambulances, hospitalizations, legal bills, some paid, some unpaid, some ongoing. My financial difficulties are, from what I can discern, par for the course for the illness.

It's an odd thing, talking with my girlfriend about my disability, the ways in which I'm unable to work in any sort of a conventional setting, because of how socially limited I am, and to know that we both see and recognize my limitations. It's an odd thing, to contemplate what that might mean for our future.

"It's like you have supernatural powers," she says, too, because she recognizes that my mind is also capable of more than many people's, in terms of my ability to process huge amounts of information, to manage complexity and plan for every outcome, to read and sense people's intentions and emotions accurately, to see what others miss. It's not just that I have a serious, stigmatized mental illness and am therefore deficient—it's more, from what I can tell, that I'm different.

I experience emotion differently than someone who is neurotypical; I pick up on the frequency of others' emotional landscapes around me. I think of this as similar to how an MRI produces visible images of what, without magneticism, without radio waves, would be imperceptible to the human eye. I think of this, too, as similar to how animals seem to communicate.

When I walked up a steep incline, up the side of Pikes Peak in Colorado, a stranger's dog stopped every time I lagged on the ascent. I'd just been released from the hospital a few weeks before, and I was in no condition for the trail.

"He's waiting for you," she said to me, friendly and also struggling to get her large black dog to focus on the path ahead, instead of checking in on me. Once I'd really given up, her large black dog no longer seemed worried, loping up the trail without turning back to check.

I think of myself as similar to a weather vane, swaying and pointing in the direction of the winds around me. I grew up in a house filled with toxic rage. As a still-developing photograph soaking in chemical baths, after those years and years of being submerged in such toxicity, your sensitivity changes to things like kindness and cruelty. As a photograph plunged in citric acid too late, overexposed, the image that results changes, too, forever frozen in the wrong moment in time.

Besides my father, who tends not to believe in things like mental illness, psychology, or doctors' visits, and who therefore has been immune to things like diagnosis, each person in my direct family has been diagnosed with at least one medically rare, genetically predisposed condition, most of which strike 1 percent of the population or less.

Early-onset Alzheimer's, bipolar, clinical depression, anxiety, PTSD, schizophrenia, Hodgkin's lymphoma concurring with another cancer, a blood-clotting disorder causing a massive pulmonary embolism—all this and more, among just four people. For my sisters and myself, this happened by our mid-thirties, when most other people are beginning their own families. With my illness, particularly, given its chronic nature, given significantly higher rates of institutionalization, criminalization, and homelessness, the public and the private cross.

So often our urge to simplify, to focus on issues in isolation, ignores the ways in which mental illnesses travel in constellations—how they can cluster together, and also how they can cluster in families. If there's any lesson I've taken away, it's that here in the U.S., at least, especially without broad social support, suffering so much illness takes a huge toll on a family. The shock waves can nearly wipe you out.

*   *   *

Unlike other illnesses, people with schizophrenia fare better in developing countries than they do in places like the U.S. It isn't clear why this is—whether it's due to social or cultural factors or something else, and how. These reversals from our expectations fascinate me, though—they show us how little we understand.

In some developing countries, according to research by Professor Alan Rosen, high-functioning people with psychoses are seen as shamans—a stark contrast to the ways in which people with schizophrenia are characterized here.

"See, we should live in Pakistan," my girlfriend tells me.

"I like that we don't play games," she says, too. Neither of us has patience for nonsense. We both, I think, take stock in our time apart, of what and why we value each other.

In her absence I miss rubbing softness and moisture into her eczema-prone skin on cold winter nights, playing at being her lotion wali, covering the same bodyscape as her waxing wali back home. I miss sheer physical presence more than anything else, more than activity or gesture. She has simple needs. I am simple in what I can offer, simple in what I require. Kindness. That's it.

Our day-to-day life is so small, insignificant, in the ways of most people's. On eventful days, after she gets treatment for a health condition of her own, we do odd things like practice stabbing each other with EpiPens. Her condition is one that typically affects children of three or four years old—her doctor hasn't seen it in adults before.

My illness, too, seems one of time. I don't experience time the way others do. The traumas of my past are real as ever, as anything, because they were never resolved. I'd frontloaded my life with caretaking, where most experience that shift from being cared for to vice versa only now, as they approach middle age.

For me past, present, and future blend together. Answers for lifelong mysteries are slowly unfolding now—why I always felt different, why I so often felt bullied and misunderstood, why I had conflict where others were able to sidestep, why each worsening of my mother's condition, each negative interaction with family, came with such turmoil and personal cost attached. Now, when most of my peers are beginning a new life, rather than receiving answers to old questions.

Health conditions are an inevitable part of life, of aging. Compared to most, my life has been lived largely backward. The question I sometimes wonder now is whether there's enough of a pause, from chronic, invisible illness, from its chaotic wake, for everything else to occur. All the space that is living.

12

FUTURITY

When I was young, I never envisioned myself on this earth past my twenties. I didn't know why—I just knew that futurity didn't seem part of my inheritance. Most in this country are confronted with the realities of mortality as fully formed adults, not while still growing into their sense of self. As I grew, so did my sense of surrounding decline, mortality, chaos, and loss, and so the natural order of things seemed reversed.

I've experienced how extremely disabling my condition is. I'm aware of the statistics. More than that, I'm aware of why my condition lends itself to those statistics. I can understand fully why most with my condition end up jobless—the *Atlantic* cites an 85 percent unemployment rate for schizophrenia, and I've seen higher rates cited, as well. I understand why joblessness is only the first concern, linked to homelessness.

I understand why people with my condition can get stuck in a cycle of hospitalizations, incarceration, and shelters, existing in a shadow universe. People without the illness don't see the linkages, how one aspect leads to the next to the next, to various forms of institutionalization. They don't see how exhausting moving from one consequence of illness to another can be. People without the illness, outside of the medical profession, and even many within it, have almost no sense of what schizophrenia means, of what it looks like, feels like, much less how to coexist successfully with those with the condition.

As I experience symptoms in real time, amplified and more noticeable in periods when my health worsens, I can research how those symptoms are part of my illness. I have names for things now. It's exhausting, this cataloguing of the loss of my health, and yet it affirms for me what I've felt my entire life—how different I am from those around me, and how this difference has caused friction and conflict nearly always.

Alogia, for example: a lack or poverty of speech, one of the so-called negative symptoms of my illness. I've experienced this my whole life without having a name for it. This has only grown more pronounced for me, to the point that engaging verbally with others, beyond my partner, is grueling. With her I can prattle on so she forgets, until we're in the company of others, that around others, I barely speak at all.

When I used to attend, with my partner's friends, doughnut Sundays, I stayed silent, noticeably silent, embarrassingly silent, during conversation. Her friends didn't know that these occasions were often the only social engagement I'd had in a week's time, if not longer—and that this absence of social engagement isn't accidental, but purposeful, one of the only ways I can find to ameliorate my condition, despite the tremendous loneliness that accompanies such social isolation.

My silence has always been a problem. Others have attributed negative intent on my behalf, assuming my silence is selfish, that I am purposely keeping back my thoughts for myself, when in reality, I am often too afraid to speak, not sure when and where to insert myself into the conversation. Like a novice trying to surf, my movements are uncoordinated—I'm not quite sure when to throw myself up onto my elbows, push and stand, and so instead I lie passively, while the waves of conversation lap and tide, and I miss every appropriate window to enter midstream.

More than simple fear, I oftentimes am simply unable to verbalize—a symptom of my illness that has become more pronounced. Being robbed of the ability to speak means lacking the social graces of small talk. It means missing out on connection. It means being unable to voice inner objections.

The negative and cognitive symptoms of my illness are what are so disabling. These symptoms, the ones no one talks about, recognizes, or knows, are the ones that render me nearly nonfunctional so frequently. The positive symptoms—the hallucinations, the delusions—are what keep me terrified of what could be.

I have capabilities still. I am a good listener, a good observer of the character of others—a trait of survival, I think, honed over a lifetime. When you're not able to speak easily, you're at the mercy of each person with whom you engage. Others tend to fill those silences with their own words, their own assumptions, tend to insert their own wills. You become a mirror, where the other sees their own reflection and their own desires.

I am, too, a good editor of others' work. When you've learned most of what you know of the world through reading, you have an understanding of what a proper narrative should contain. When you've spent a lifetime trying to translate your experience of the world to something others can understand, impossible though that task might be, it's easy to edit the work of others, to bring forward the coherence and meaning.

And I'm a good teacher of certain things, of things that are technical, precise. I'm good at understanding underlying structures. I'm a good teacher to those willing to be taught by me.

I have abilities, still. I can still learn, both in global, conceptual ways and in details. But the abilities I lack—in the social realm, in the verbal realm, in the cognitive realm, in the real-time world—make daily life virtually impossible to navigate independently. Conflict, criticism, and negativity derail me. Managing interaction with different personalities simultaneously is nearly impossible. I can exist on paper, but existing in real life is another matter.

Social aspects have always been the greatest difficulty I've faced. My illness affects my social cognition. It feels as though those parts of my brain are absent, or don't function as they would in others. I've long felt my barriers to work have not been my capacity to do the work, but rather my ability to manage the sorts of human connection that are necessary to work, in different ways. People don't generally like me, and I can sense that. They don't generally trust me. There's nearly always some point at which I say something wrong, do something wrong, think about things wrongly. The feeling is often mutual, as well. I often observe actions and emotions that others don't, because I'm focused on the particularities. I see the small things.

I am, at this point, utterly reliant on those around me, even as I am capable of doing quite a bit—if, and only if, the conditions are right. My capabilities shift, depending on circumstance. When my partner is coming home and I know she's had a busy day, I can rouse myself to make seafood chowder and pasta with pan-roasted vegetables. When she's out of town, I can barely stir the energy or care to open a can of corn to eat. In her absence I don't venture into the outer world, don't interact with anyone for days or weeks.

I would be unable to climb, the one activity in which I still engage, without my partner, to whom it's fundamental that we continue climbing. But with her I'm capable of certain things. I've been able to teach her nearly everything I know of climbing technique, of safety, so that now, with her ability to work out or climb daily, an ability I've lost, with her superior fitness, she surpasses me.

I can exist well with my partner because I understand innately how she moves through the world, and because she reacts with kindness, always. But existing with others, strangers, and those not as kind is another matter.

This is a lot of stress to place on any one person. Because my partner doesn't view things as I do, she doesn't feel this stress. But I do. The difference is stark.

On my own, sensory overload prevents me from doing simple things. I can't ride public transit, or be in public spaces or around crowds for long. I impose isolation on myself, as a way to avoid the friction that inevitably results from social interaction. This isolation is effective, but unbelievably fatiguing, in its own way. The incredible loneliness of my condition overwhelms.

As my condition changes, my capability to do the actual work changes, as well. It becomes harder and harder to exert myself or my will. Apathy, lack of motivation, difficulty starting tasks—these are all symptoms of my illness, and I experience them at a level far beyond what these casual phrases imply. I can't concentrate anymore—often can't read a book, can almost never watch TV or consume media, or relax in the ways most take for granted.

My symptoms make little sense. On a good day, if shown a page of text, I can read it far faster than your average person, almost instantaneously. On a bad day, I can read one paragraph over and over without understanding, or I can be too overwhelmed to even look at the page.

I have memory loss. Nightmares. Each day half my day is gone by the time I've greeted it. After a lifetime of sleeping on a different schedule than anyone else, up until the wee hours of the morning every night, medication knocks me out routinely, for twelve-plus hours at a stretch.

My condition is debilitating. Beyond words, beyond language. It can take me days at a stretch, if not longer, to recover from social interaction, or even from existing in the outside world. During this time I can do essentially nothing beyond lying down, waiting to feel better. Sheer physical fatigue takes over, as does mental distortion. These distorted thoughts can preoccupy me for long stretches of time. Accompanying this distortion is my inability to place myself in time.

Nearly every day I'm consumed by fear of something terrible happening, even if the specifics change. I can feel my brain changing, deteriorating. I can feel my relationship to myself changing. I feel loss ever-present.

This is what I wish others understood of my illness, as well as of illnesses such as early-onset Alzheimer's: that change is the constant. There is so much flux in condition from one day to the next, that it's nearly impossible to accurately capture the full picture. That personality change is an aspect of these sorts of illnesses.

I know my illness will likely shorten my life span, by estimates of ten to twenty-five years. I know people with my illness have significantly elevated rates of suicide. I know psychosis especially lends itself to such scenarios. I know first-degree family members are likely to suffer cognitive impairments and deficits, as well. This matches my experience within my family, where my difficulties communicating intersected with my family members' failure to understand.

Research will reveal, too, how much exposure to stress, especially earlier in life, contributes to the development of schizophrenia.

I've gotten used to pretending, to hiding. To acting more capable than I feel. But as I worsen, this becomes impossible. I can't navigate the outside world independently anymore.

I think of how much my mother was able to do for so long, despite her illness, perhaps because she had no other way forward, no one to help her. I think about how with both of us, intelligence masked our conditions, so that people could mistake us, at least initially, as fully capable, perhaps even normal. I think about how despite how unable my mother was to do simple things, like sign her own name to a piece of paper and understand what she was signing, she kept working. She didn't just survive financially. She put her children through college, accumulated retirement savings, paid off her own house. She left behind resources for her family's survival.

And I think, too, about how filled her world was with fear. How lonely she was. How alone she was, without resources to turn to in society, for help. I think about her students, who didn't have a fully functioning teacher. I think about how there wasn't an alternative path—one in which she received help, in which she didn't have to be a money earner while simultaneously being unable to care for herself.

I live with similar sorts of fears now, as I once witnessed in her. Fears about how to fulfill, each day, the smallest of necessary tasks, to proceed to the next day. You move through the world differently once you're unsure of your capability to care for yourself. Life becomes consciously, acutely, about survival.

In the company of those whom I value, who value me, too, as I am, there are moments of great joy. Of relief, and of beauty. Pleasure comes in the small moments, in the textures of the everyday, in moments of health, in moments of reprieve—when, in summertime, my partner and I buy boxes full of fragrant mangos on Devon, after being elbowed aside by the auntie eager to pick out the best ones. When our kitchen accidentally overflows with bananas—banana bunches everywhere—so I spend days processing bananas, freezing them, and we visit the pleasures of drinking the iced banana shakes she grew up with as a child. When we stand on chalky mats, staring up at a problem in the gym, arms waving wildly, unlocking a new sequence. When laughing over red wine and a home-cooked meal with friends.

I'm grateful each day for what hasn't been taken from me yet, what has been preserved, even as I fear my condition may change and worsen. I've gotten sicker; who knows what the future holds. I want to keep up with my partner, to build a life together that doesn't involve holding her back. Whether this is possible is a question to which I don't have an answer, or which I'm afraid to contemplate.

Even if parts of myself deteriorate, I'm also equipped with the skills I learned in youth and beyond, in how to take care of others and myself. I'm blessed with love—the capacity to feel it deeply, to be motivated by it, and to possess and share it with someone equally aware of its worth.

I feel keenly the divide between what I want to achieve, to contribute, to do, and what's possible for me. I feel my limitations. I'm too sensitive for this world. And yet I'm here.

ACKNOWLEDGMENTS

Thank you to Roxane Gay for caring enough to help, time and again, in so many ways, and without whose assistance this work wouldn't exist in the world.

Thank you to Johanna V. Castillo for lending excellence and expertise, and for steady guidance in navigating new terrain. Thank you to Wendy Sabrozo for easing the process and making the journey a pleasant one. Thank you to Michelle Herrera Mulligan for sharing insight and encouragement, and for making this book a reality. Thank you to Min Choi for the beautiful cover design. Thank you to Melanie Iglesias Pérez, Erin Patterson, and everyone at Atria and Writers House.

Thank you to Sharon Solwitz, Kaveh Akbar, and Dr. Nush Powell, for aid in finishing grad school. Thank you to Don Platt, for leading with kindness, and to Marianne Boruch, for sharing poetic wonder. Thank you to Chris Durbin, for listening and helping. Thank you to my MFA cohort.

ACKNOWLEDGMENTS

Thank you to Ellen Usher, George Singleton, and Barbara Ensor, for help in pursuing grad school. Thank you to the Wesleyan Writers Conference, Big River Writers Conference, Cape Cod Writers Conference, and Eckerd Writers' Conference.

Thank you to Ryan for believing I could write, and supporting me in finding my way. Thank you to my sister, for supporting me in speaking. Thank you to Hannah Rahimi for friendship. Thank you to Chelsy and Basil for the same.

Thank you to mere jaanu, for home.